Missions Have Come Home to America

The Church's Cross-cultural Ministry to Ethnics

Missions Have Come Home to America

The Church's Cross-cultural Ministry to Ethnics

by

Jerry L. Appleby

Beacon Hill Press of Kansas City
Kansas City, Missouri

Permission to quote from the following copyrighted version of the Bible is
acknowledged with appreciation:

The Holy Bible, New International Version (NIV), copyright © 1973, 1978,
1984 by the International Bible Society.

10 9 8 7 6 5 (1990)

Contents

84818

Foreword

"Why is God internationalizing American cities?" Author Jerry Appleby not only raises this pertinent and timely question but addresses himself to the challenges of cross-cultural evangelism in the American context. For five years Rev. Appleby served on an international commission that studied cross-cultural ministries. As an active participant in that group, he helped to shape legislation that was recently adopted in the Church of the Nazarene respecting the multicultural church. He writes from the background of a missionary in American Samoa and a church planter and Bible college founder in Western Samoa. He also has served in multicultural work in Honolulu First and Pasadena (Calif.) Bresee Avenue Church of the Nazarene. For about three years he was the coordinator of ethnic/urban missions at the international headquarters of the Church of the Nazarene.

As an active participant in Houston '85, Consultation on Evangelizing Ethnic America, conducted by 43 denominations, Rev. Appleby brings to this discussion an understanding of ethnic ministries broader than his own denomination. The reality of this book will grip you. Barriers to cross-cultural evangelism are frankly addressed, but positive input is given in the several ethnic church-planting models described. The practical ideas put forth may start you and your church on a totally different evangelistic journey. When you have read this book you will want to do something about the missionary task at home among those of a different language, nationality, culture, or social situation. We wish for this book the widest possible readership.

—RAYMOND W. HURN
General Superintendent
Church of the Nazarene

7

1

Eyes for the Harvest

It was a winter night in New York City when a young Puerto Rican woman hurried to use the pay phone in the neighborhood bar. She ignored the slurred comments from the half-drunken patrons and went straight to the bartender to ask for change. But there was an immediate communication problem—she spoke only Spanish, and he spoke only English.

In her effort to transmit her need she became upset; her voice rose with emotion as she shouted her words, hoping to be understood. The busy bartender, not understanding her outburst, shouted back in the only language he knew. Finally, infuriated, he called the police.

When the police arrived, the uncontrolled woman continued to gesture and explain her situation in Spanish. But the police understood only English. Not knowing what to do to calm the now hysterical woman, they called an ambulance.

The ambulance attendants rushed to the bar and tried in vain to talk to the Puerto Rican woman. But they spoke only English. Feeling trapped by all the uniformed men, the woman became more frightened and outraged. In frustration, the attendants forceably wheeled her away to the psychiatric unit of a nearby urban hospital.

For three long days she lay strapped in her bed before a Spanish-speaking social worker was called in. The resulting conversation sent the social worker dashing to the Puerto Rican woman's small apartment. But she was too late—for there lay three small children, dead from thirst!

The young mother had only wanted correct change to make a phone call to her doctor. But she did not speak the language in which help was available.

When I read this newspaper article I was shaken to realize that children living in America could die because their family did not speak English. My concern deepened as I pondered this question: How many people on this continent die each day totally unprepared to meet their God because they don't speak the language in which salvation is available?

It is not enough simply to say we are interested in missions. We can no longer get by with the excuse that we are taking part in some promotion of missions. Most missionary efforts in the local church fall short. They are based either on an inadequate understanding of what missions is all about or on an appeal for pity.

The military and business management share an excellent definition of *mission:* it is the dedication of personnel and materials necessary to accomplish an objective. If all denominations would be willing to dedicate the necessary personnel and materials to the task of world evangelization, great progress would be made.

Missions is not a human concept. It did not originate in the mind of Carey, Livingstone, Schmelzenbach, or any other modern-day missionary. Neither was it a carefully thought-out concept of the apostle Paul. It is from the heart of God. It is based on the coming of Jesus to earth. He was God's great Missionary.

> For God so loved the world, that he gave his only begotten Son, that whosoever believeth in him should not perish, but have everlasting life *(John 3:16).*

This is the central missionary text, but there are more:

> For God sent not his Son into the world to condemn the world; but that the world through him might be saved (*John 3:17*).

> God was in Christ, reconciling the world unto himself (*2 Cor. 5:19*).

> He is the propitiation for our sins: and not for ours only, but also for the sins of the whole world (*1 John 2:2*).

> Behold the Lamb of God, which taketh away the sin of the world (*John 1:29*).

The redemption of the whole world was and is God's plan. The "whosoever" in John 3:16 is the crucial word for the church in mission today. The transparent design of God was that by sending His Son to the world all people might know forgiveness of sins. He is concerned equally for all races. Peter spoke of it when he preached:

> Of a truth I perceive that God is no respecter of persons: but in every nation he that feareth him, and worketh righteousness, is accepted with him (*Acts 10:34-35*).

Acts continues with the truth that:

> [He] hath made of one blood all nations of men . . . that they should seek the Lord, if haply they might feel after him, and find him (*17:26-27*).

If you have thought that missions is simply the sending of missionaries overseas, read these scriptures over again. Missions is carrying into effect the divine purpose and project set by God from the foundation of the world. That purpose is stated most clearly in Matthew's account of the Great Commission:

> All power is given unto me in heaven and in earth. Go ye therefore, and teach all nations . . . and, lo, I am with you alway, even unto the end of the world (*Matt. 28:18-20*).

Discipling all nations—that is what it is all about. What a task! We are not just to win them, but to disciple them.

Jesus performed a great miracle in the feeding of the 5,000, and each writer of the Gospels chose to give his version. The spiritual lesson of this story does not take away from the tremendous significance it played in the history of Jesus on earth.

The Twelve had just returned from their mission into the surrounding cities. John the Baptist had recently been killed. Obviously, Herod was growing more hostile toward Jesus and His ministry.

The disciples needed a retreat. Surely they deserved a little time to get alone with Jesus and reflect on the recent happenings. So they got in a boat to travel the six miles across the sea. They forgot that the people could walk the eight miles around the edge of the sea faster than they could row across. When they arrived on the other side, they found the crowd again. Jesus decided He would postpone the retreat and give some more time to the people. The subsequent miracle has a missionary lesson for us who would have eyes for the ethnic harvest of today. Jesus taught His disciples (including us) three basic lessons concerning cross-cultural church planting:

1. The disciple must have eyes to see the harvest.
2. The disciple must have compassion for the lost.
3. The disciple must have power for action.

A. *Eyes to See*

As evening approached, the disciples came to him and said, "This is a remote place, and it's already getting late. Send the crowds away, so they can go to the villages and buy themselves some food." Jesus replied, "They do not need to go away. You give them something to eat." "We have here only five loaves of bread and two fish," they answered (*Matt. 14:15-17, NIV*).

Jesus' vision in difficult circumstances was an example set before the disciples. Certainly the Twelve needed an example. They were having great difficulty with their vision. The preceding verse (14) reads, "When Jesus . . . saw a large crowd . . ." He had no problem with His vision. He provided a contrast to a group of disciples who could not see the needs of the multitude and hence did not share in His decision to stay and meet their needs.

All disciples share in the first problem displayed by the Twelve, a **self-centered vision.** In facing the needs of today's church in the United States, it is easy to be selfish about our approach. Jesus' disciples wanted to go ahead with their retreat. They felt this time was theirs and should not be disturbed by outsiders.

Our time, our buildings, our leadership, our money, and —above all—our Lord must be shared if the ethnic harvest of America is to be reaped. This is not easy! "Our" resources must be God's possessions. He must be in control as we allow time, buildings, leadership, money, and Christ himself to be used for the salvation of those He chooses. The cataract of selfishness must be removed in order to clear our vision!

Closely linked to selfishness is the problem of a **prejudiced vision.** It does not take a Bible scholar to recognize that Jesus was standing in the midst of an ethnic harvest for the Jews of that day when He exhorted His disciples, "I tell you, open your eyes and look at the fields! They are ripe for harvest" (John 4:35, NIV). Jews looked on these Samaritans as mongrels. They treated them with contempt. Jesus must have taken His disciples to Samaria intentionally for this lesson. They needed to see that the harvest did not lie only within their culture, race, and socioeconomic group. Their part in God's plan of salvation for the world could not be defined in their terms. It could not be put in a box.

Two events in the Book of Acts contributed to bringing this to pass: (1) The death of Stephen (Acts 7) scattered the

Church from its central location (Acts 8); and (2) the Council at Jerusalem (Acts 15) made official the open evangelism of Gentile Christians without the weight of the Jewish religious rules.

History proved that as they carried this plan to the civilized world of that time, many other nations and people heard and believed.

The West has been a favored people. We have learned to have pride of race, learning, wealth, power, and much more. This superior feeling has many times kept us from identifying with neighbors who may have customs different from ours.

Yes, there will be differences in physiognomy, speech, dress, customs, and mode of living. But these are superficial differences. All people have feelings of hate and love. All know sorrow and joy. All harbor prejudice. All sin and need a Savior.

Many of those who live in our neighborhood, whose customs, ways, and color may be different from ours, could be the same as those to whom we sent missionaries just a few years ago. They are the product of mission dollars over centuries. What an opportunity we have to display the attitude of Christ by loving them as much when they are in our neighborhood as we do when they are overseas. Prejudice can be broken and replaced by a Christlike love for all.

Jesus' disciples also had a **clouded vision.** They could not see clearly the full plan that Jesus had in His coming to earth.

Dr. Raymond Bakke, urban sociologist, in a recent speech, asked two very important questions: "Why is God urbanizing the world?" and "Why is God internationalizing the cities of North America?" ("Significance of Urbanization for World Missions," mission leaders meeting, May 12, 1982). Signs point out that God is in action to bring the nations of the world to us. This does not negate our responsibility to go to the world. It does, however, emphasize a need for massive church planting and missionary effort in the United States. Some would argue, "Why spend so much time and effort with ethnics here when there is so much work to do among our own people?" There are several reasons:

1. No country has prospered that has been selfish with the gospel. No denomination has prospered that has not aggressively taken the gospel to others cross-culturally.

2. The Bible is clear that light not shared soon becomes darkness. The Israelites thought they could store the manna provided for them in the desert. Soon, however, they discovered worms were breeding in the hoarded blessings.

3. Churches that are inward looking, without a fresh, clean vision of the harvest, are dying.

Oh, for a fresh, clean, clear vision to sweep over the churches of America! May we lift up our eyes and look beyond our narrow borders and local interests and learn to share the vision of Christ for all mankind. "Where there is no vision, the people perish" (Prov. 29:18).

Certainly the first lesson taught by Jesus to us who are His disciples is a need for eyes free from disease and obstruction to see the harvest that is all around us.

B. *A Heart to Feel*

> When Jesus landed and saw a large crowd, he had compassion on them and healed their sick *(Matt. 14:14, NIV)*.

The commonly accepted definition of "compassion" is a feeling of pity, or sympathy. *The Random House Dictionary* defines compassion as "a feeling of deep sympathy and sorrow for another who is stricken by suffering or misfortune, *accompanied by a strong desire to alleviate the pain or remove the cause*" (emphasis mine). This corresponds with the Greek meaning of the word translated "compassion." It carries a direct feeling of "suffering together with."

Matthew also uses this word when he describes one of Jesus' preaching tours: "When he saw the crowds, he had compassion on them, because they were harassed and helpless, like sheep without a shepherd" (Matt. 9:36, NIV).

Jesus had adequate reason to look on the crowd with compassion. They were carrying (as implied in the Greek) burdens too heavy to bear and were thrown down as in cruel treatment or oppression. Jesus not only suffered in His compassion, He was willing to do something to help. He was called "a man of sorrows, and acquainted with grief" (Isa. 53:3) because He carried the sorrows of others on the Cross. "In all their affliction he was afflicted" (63:9). Jesus' compassion stirred Him to the very depths of His soul—and moved Him to action. He could not look on the multitude with compassion, feel their hurt, and shut His heart to any appeal for help.

I sat in a church service and watched several Cambodians go forward to receive Christ as their Savior. I knelt with them as they told their stories of horror through an interpreter. One told of leaving Cambodia in a hurry, leaving behind his wife and children. He had selfishly escaped, not thinking of their safety. He felt sure they were killed or at least suffering under the communist government. I will always remember his question: "Do you think God can forgive me for what I have done?"

Another told how he had hid in a hole in the ground with his wife and child. The government had decided to kill all educated people, and he was a schoolteacher. The pain, suffering, hunger, thirst, and bitterness were something I had never known. It was very hard to identify with the hatred this young man felt toward the guards that had killed his relatives and the government that had made his escape to Thailand necessary.

The young lady kneeling there was alone. Her husband had died at the hands of the enemy soldiers. She bravely chose to escape with a large band of people who were planning the trip through the forest that lay between Cambodia and Thailand. None had any assurance they would make it alive, but all hoped for the best. As the days wore on, all in the group became more and more restless, including the children. Her baby was only a few months old and was often hungry. One particular night as they were traveling through a heavily patrolled section her baby began to cry. It seemed all her frantic efforts were failing to stop him. As the others pressured her to control the noise, she faced a hard choice. Would she risk the lives of all these who had come so far to find freedom, or would she silence this one to whom she had given birth such a short time before? Her question at the altar echoed the young man's: "Do you think God will forgive me for taking the life of my baby?"

What a joy it was to see the forgiveness of Jesus wipe away the guilt and sorrow in these hearts. What a joy it was to have the privilege of making these people my friends as I tried to have a part in discipling them.

The mental and physical suffering in Cambodia, Vietnam, Laos, and so many other nations of the world is well documented in newspapers, books, magazines, and personal accounts. We must always stand firm as a nation, a church, and individuals who will not tolerate injustices such as those seen in these nations. To allow these actions to go unheeded is a cruelty in itself.

However, nothing can compare with the cruelty we inflict when we allow even *one* to remain in the grasp of sin. The impersonal gods of the East can offer philosophies and rules that guide one to a better life-style. They can be a path that has a number of good points. But they do not offer the Way, the only Way. To bring one to Christ is to offer the continuous, sufficient Way that opens the door to life itself. We surely would in no way allow our material, mental, and emotional needs to block the ultimate goal of leading these souls to Christ.

We have the solution. Jesus said: "They do not need to go away. You give them something to eat" (Matt. 14:16, NIV).

C. *Power to Act*

A minister I knew spent countless hours in his study praying for his people. None could doubt his ability to see their needs. It seemed obvious that he felt their hurts. But there were very few visible results. As Christ's disciples, it is not enough to open our eyes and develop hearts of compassion without actions empowered by the Holy Spirit. Emotion is never a satisfactory substitute for real compassion, which involves actively meeting a need.

In the feeding of the 5,000, Jesus no doubt had a plan of action which involved faith-filled disciples jumping in to carry out every detail. But the disciples made excuses. These excuses are similar to the ones that plague the Church today:

1. Not Enough Money

Jesus had asked them to feed the people. Philip's reply was, "That would take eight months of a man's wages! Are we to go and spend that much on bread and give it to them to eat?" (Mark 6:37, NIV).

A man from an ethnic minority group came up to me and explained that they could not evangelize their people in the United States because they did not have the finances necessary to do so. I responded to him as Jesus did to His disciples in instructing them before they went out on their first evangelistic trip: "The harvest is plentiful, but the workers are few. Ask the Lord of the harvest, therefore, to send out workers into his harvest field" (Luke 10:2, NIV). Finances are not the major concern of the Church today. We must have laborers. We can use the financial excuse for years and watch the harvest go to waste.

2. Only a Lad

Andrew had his excuse: "Here is a boy with five small

barley loaves and two small fish, but how far will they go among so many?" (John 6:9, NIV).

The Greek makes it clear that this was a small boy, as indicated in so many of the paintings of this miracle. Could it be that Andrew was as discouraged by the size of the boy as he was with the small amount of food?

God has chosen to use "little people" throughout the Bible. The child Samuel; David, youngest of Jesse's sons; Gideon, "the least in my father's house" (Judg. 6:15); the little maid who helped Nathan; the little colt upon which Jesus rode—these are but a few examples of this truth.

> But God chose the foolish things of the world to shame the wise; God chose the weak things of the world to shame the strong. He chose the lowly things of this world and the despised things—and the things that are not—to nullify the things that are, so that no one may boast before him (1 Cor. 1:27-29, NIV).

Often the ethnic challenge of the United States is picked up by laymen who have largely been unused or unheralded in the past. God has not chosen always to use the well-known, multitalented individual. And why not? All Christians are what they are because God has chosen to take their small talents and use them in a mighty way. It is really nothing new or strange for God to use the "little lads" of the Christian world to bring about a revival among the "many nations" of the United States. "Little is much when God is in it."

3. Jesus Could Do It Himself

The excuse of passing the buck back to the Lord is not pointed out in the Scripture, but it seems implicit. If Jesus could break the bread and fish and make enough for the 5,000 men, plus women and children, could He not make the food float out to the people so they could eat? Why was this miracle not possible? The disciples must have been thinking something like that.

Jesus could have fed the multitude without the little lad or the disciples, but He chose not to do so. Jesus did not have to use the disciples. However, His plan of action through His ministry was to use people to take the "bread" to the multitudes.

> And he directed the people to sit down on the grass. Taking the five loaves and the two fish and looking up to heaven, he gave thanks and broke the loaves. Then he gave them to the disciples, and the disciples gave them to the people (*Matt. 14:19, NIV*).

Loaves, disciples, multitude—it has not changed today. We still must be the ones designated to carry the gospel to the many people of the United States. No matter who we are or where we are from, we cannot escape this responsibility. God has chosen to place us between the bread and the multitude.

We have spoken very little about the empowering for service. We all have experienced action undertaken in our own power. Planting churches cross-culturally is as difficult as any task in the Kingdom. We dare not undertake this task without prayer accompanied by fasting. There must not only be prayer and fasting by the individual (a necessity), but we must also solicit the prayer and fasting support of all groups that will join us. This is a matter of no little consequence.

God has a way of dividing the good from the bad, the up from the down, the worker from the slothful, the live from the dead. In the matter of responsibility for the ethnic harvest He has placed all Christians in the position of either the obstructionist or the loyal helper. There is no third position. The "bread" must be given to the multitudes who are invading our shores. We have been entrusted with a great responsibility. The church, and every individual member, must commit itself to taking the Bread of Life, with all possible speed, to a multitude of souls that are dying for lack of it.

2

Closing Missions' Backdoors

The ABC television announcer for the 1984 Summer Olympics surprised some of us when he commented that every nation represented in the games was also represented among the residents of Los Angeles.

We drink coffee from Latin America. We wear cotton shirts woven in India and suits from England and Scotland. Japan furnishes us cars, TVs, stereos, and cameras. We eat pizza and spaghetti native to Italy. It surprises us to realize this is happening in our United States. Let's consider a few facts:

1. The United States has the second-largest Black population of any country in the world (Nigeria is first).
2. America has the fourth-largest Spanish population in the world. We may overtake Argentina, the third, this decade.
3. The United States is next to Poland in Polish population. Chicago is the second-largest Polish city.
4. The United States has the largest Jewish population in the world.
5. In the 1980 census only 30 percent of the residents in the U.S. checked "white American."

6. The largest ethnic groups in America are German, Black, and Hispanic, in that order.
7. There are more Hispanics in the United States than there are people in Canada.
8. In the five counties around Los Angeles, there are 4.5 million Hispanics. This makes it the second-largest Spanish population center in the world, next only to Mexico City.
9. In the Houston school system 80 percent of the students are Black, Asian, or Hispanic.
10. Los Angeles is now 72 percent non-Anglo-American.
11. Houston and Los Angeles may soon replace New York as the main port of entry for newcomers to the U.S.A.
12. There are more Jews in New York City than in Tel Aviv.
13. New York City is the second-largest Puerto Rican city.
14. Twenty-five major cities in the United States have a majority ethnic. By the year 2,000 it is predicted that 50 major cities will be predominantly ethnic "minority."
15. The United States receives 1.1 million newcomers each year:

400,000	Legal immigrants
600,000	Undocumented
	(this is a net figure;
	1.1 million arrive and
	500,000 leave each year)
60,000	Refugees
40,000	Special emphasis
1,100,000	Immigrants

IMMIGRATION'S EFFECT

Immigration has had a profound effect on the complexion of our nation. It has not only guided our past but also set the course for the future.

IMMIGRATION
1820-1957

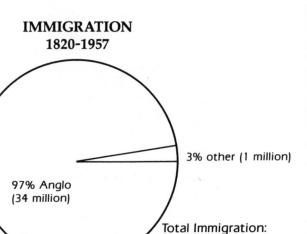

3% other (1 million)

97% Anglo
(34 million)

Total Immigration:
35 Million

Chart 1

IMMIGRATION
1960-1984
(Not including refugees and illegal immigrants)

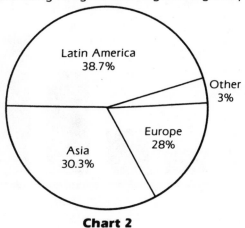

Latin America
38.7%

Other
3%

Europe
28%

Asia
30.3%

Chart 2

Between 1820 and 1957 approximately 35 million immigrants were admitted into the United States. But, as you will notice on the accompanying chart (see chart 1), 34 million of these were from European countries. During these years the blending process happened quickly as the language difficulties were solved.

However, in the period 1960-84 a different picture developed. Almost 39 percent of the immigrants were from Latin America, 30.3 percent were from Asia, while only 28 percent were from European nations (see chart 2).

These figures are compounded by three factors:

1. Immigration has drastically increased in the last few decades. In the 1930s, slightly more than ½ million immigrants came to the United States annually. In the 1970s, however, almost 4 million legal immigrants were admitted. By changing the number legally admitted, we have allowed additional millions into our land (see chart 3).

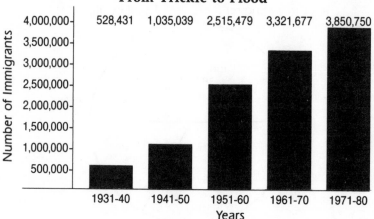

IMMIGRANTS:
From Trickle to Flood

Chart 3

REFUGEES
Approximate Numbers, 1961-1984

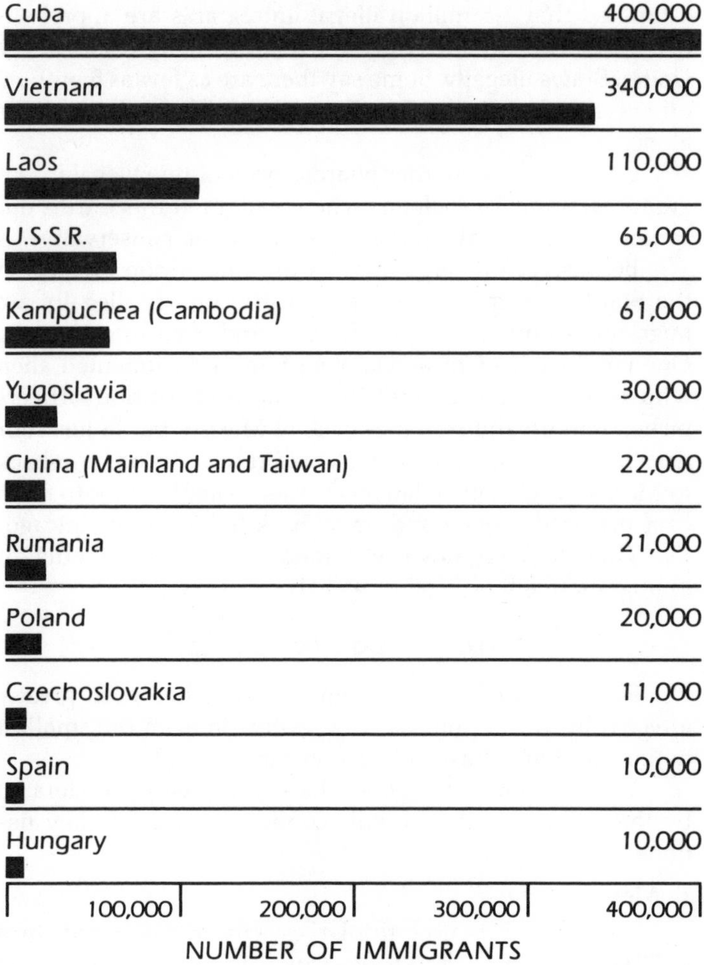

Cuba	400,000
Vietnam	340,000
Laos	110,000
U.S.S.R.	65,000
Kampuchea (Cambodia)	61,000
Yugoslavia	30,000
China (Mainland and Taiwan)	22,000
Rumania	21,000
Poland	20,000
Czechoslovakia	11,000
Spain	10,000
Hungary	10,000

100,000   200,000   300,000   400,000

NUMBER OF IMMIGRANTS

Chart 3A

25

2. Immigrants were admitted under various refugee acts between 1961 and 1984 (see chart 3A).

3. Illegal entry into our country is on the rise. It is now estimated that 1.5 million illegal immigrants are apprehended each year. No one really knows how many reside in the United States illegally. Some say there are as few as 5 million; others say there are 12 million undocumented Mexicans alone.

Off the record, border guards speak of two illegal immigrants escaping for each one who is caught. If this is true, our earlier statements about illegal entry are too conservative.

Because of the large number of immigration officials in the Southwest, many coming into the country illegally are migrating to other areas in the U.S. and even into Canada. One employer in Chicago spoke of an undocumented alien who was working in his shop. The immigration officers picked him up and sent him back to Mexico, but in just four days he was back on the job. He had received a free trip back to Mexico to visit his relatives. It was a simple thing to cross over the border again and travel back to his job in Chicago.

There are very few communities free from the touch of immigration, either legal or illegal.

THE FOREIGN INFLUENCE

Since World War I the United States has been greatly affected by world politics. Now, events in even the smallest nation can have drastic effects on each of us.

The immigration problem has been greatly accelerated by the political and economic conditions of a few key nations.

1. Mexico

Mexico City is now the largest city in the world. In a 1920 sociological study, Mexico City was not even mentioned in the top 10 cities for future growth. It is, however, growing at a rate of 80,000 per month—about 1 million per year. This is the equivalent of one new Los Angeles or Chicago inside the city limits of Mexico City every three years. A recent study showed the median age of Mexico City at 14.2 years. With the present population set at 20 million, approximately 9-10 million are under 14 years of age.

Mexico must provide 1 million new jobs each year to keep up with Mexico City's growth alone. In a recent year (the best year ever) 400,000 new jobs were produced, largely through oil production. Where are the other 600,000 people going to get a job? How will they be able to make a living? Many of them are seeking out the nearest border, crossing as many times as necessary to obtain entry, and blending into the work force. Earthquakes and other national disasters only quicken the flow into the United States and Canada.

Although government legislation is aimed at slowing down this flow, it is doubtful if many residents of Mexico City will be discouraged from escaping the poor air, water, and sanitation facing them in their home. Because of this and other facts, the Hispanic population of the United States continues to increase. By 1990 it is estimated that Hispanics will outnumber Blacks.

Mentioned earlier was the tremendous concentration of Spanish-speaking people in and around Los Angeles. If all non-Hispanics were removed from the five counties around Los Angeles, those remaining would still constitute the second-largest city in America.

A recent survey, conducted to better equip an evangelistic campaign in Los Angeles, found that nearly 25,000 Hispanics claimed to be evangelical. That is, about ½ of 1 percent of 4.5 million Hispanics are evangelical Christians. Almost all Latin capitals of the world claim at least 1 percent evangelicals. Could it be that the Los Angeles area is the most unevangelized Hispanic city in the "Latin world"? Does the

United States house the greatest Hispanic mission field in the world?

2. Latin America

Developments over the last few years have proven the effect Latin America is certain to have on immigration. Already thousands are arriving from El Salvador. It is no longer unusual to find people who recognize the difference between Mexican and El Salvadoran cultures. El Salvadoran churches are springing up all over the United States.

If El Salvador, Nicaragua, or any other Central American country develops into a trouble spot, there could be more and more illegal attempts to enter our country by its people.

3. The Philippines

The Philippines remains number two in legal immigration to the United States. A surprising fact is that it also is number two in illegal immigration. Tagalog, Ilacano, and other dialects are spoken in communities all across America.

When MacArthur left the Philippines during World War II, the Japanese entered and occupied the Ilacano District. Much persecution of the Filipinos followed. When the United States returned, the Ilacanos were allowed to have first choice regarding coming to America. Because of this, Ilacano is the dialect spoken by large sections of the populace of Honolulu, Los Angeles, Chicago, New York, and many other cities.

The evangelical church continues to grow at a rapid rate in the Philippines. It seems only reasonable that a great number of Christian Filipinos are immigrating to the United States. Yet few denominations are starting large numbers of Filipino churches.

The backdoor of missions is open wide among the Filipinos. We are winning them in Manila and losing them in Chicago, Los Angeles, and New York. Everything we have done to evangelize the Philippines must be done in the metropolitan areas of the United States.

4. Southeast Asia

Almost three-quarters of a million Southeast Asian refugees have arrived in the United States since 1975. They have come mainly from Vietnam, Cambodia, and Laos. Because of the nature of their plight, they are of particular interest. Some have suffered great tragedy because of the trip here. Thousands lost their lives on the unseaworthy boats used to escape Vietnam. Of this flotilla there seems no end.

War has been the problem in Cambodia. Very little publicity is given to this war, yet the refugee camps remain full and overflowing. As late as 1984, the one-day record was set for escapees into Thailand. Great revival continues in these refugee camps and in the training centers in the Philippines. A growing number of churches are receiving refugees who are in various stages of discipleship training.

The exciting aspect of the Southeast Asian work in America is that the revival fires also burn among the churches that are actively evangelizing these open people. The Southern Baptists are leading in this effort. The Church of the Nazarene has seen about 75 Southeast Asian works in various stages of development start since 1981. The receptivity level seems to be high. Secondary migration, which takes place often, does not seem to slow the evangelizing process.

Although we can look for the flow to subside from Southeast Asia, there are still good prospects for evangelical work here. There are thousands in the refugee camps, and they must be located somewhere.

5. South Korea

Korea has the largest church in the world. Christian churches there are witnessing some of the most rapid growth in the world. Koreans continue to enter the United States in large numbers, and it seems obvious that Korea is sending many Christians here. Korean churches are starting in the U.S. both denominationally and independently. It is not uncommon for a group of Koreans to come and bring their pastor with them. Korean churches seem prone to find a church in which they feel comfortable, and then share·facilities.

Evangelistic possibilities are limitless, since they surround themselves with much prayer and seemingly endless effort. New works are only limited by the number of workers that can be trained. (It should be said at this point, however, that one should follow all the procedures suggested by immigration officials in bringing prospective workers from overseas. Sometimes it is easy to cut corners and get a pastor here quickly; however, in the long run it will not pay off. A delay will be better than a bad reputation with immigration, which may cause trouble in the future.)

6. China

It is impossible to predict the impact on America that will be felt when Hong Kong is turned over to the mainland Chinese in 1997. Companies are already pulling out resources. Some are totally relocating. Many individuals are sending money regularly to New York and West Coast banks, anticipating the need for a quick relocation.

The church must also be poised to receive an influx of immigrants that may develop in the years prior to and following 1997. It is possible that as many as 1,000 new Chinese churches will be needed in California alone. Other U.S. Chinese centers will be equally affected—New York and Chicago, for instance. Present Chinese communities will certainly be welcoming points for newcomers.

Wise denominations will educate Anglo pastors in these geographical areas. Multiple use of facilities might be a possibility.

Local Response

The idea of America as a "melting pot" is almost as old as the nation itself. In *Letters from an American Farmer,* M. G. Jean de Crèvecoeur gave this late-18th-century opinion: "He is an American, who leaving behind him all his ancient prejudices and manners, receives new ones from the new mode of life he has embraced . . . Here individuals of all nations are melted into a new race of men."

In 1909 Israel Zangwill commented, "America is God's crucible, the great melting pot where all races are melting and reforming."

Even with the changing tide of America's immigration, many Americans still feel that cultural and ethnic differences should be eliminated. It is their opinion that we cannot exist as a nation as long as different viewpoints and languages exist. Some would promote massive efforts to eliminate foreign customs and nationalism, which they fear would undermine loyalty to the United States.

However, school systems alone indicate that we are beyond that point in our history. Most public schools in America have children from homes where a language other than English is spoken. In many school systems 10-25 different languages are represented by the children and their families. It is not unusual for Anglo children to have Hispanic, Korean, Cambodian, or Afghan playmates. The difference between this wave of immigration and past waves are twofold:

1. Sheer numbers have allowed people to congregate and exist for long periods without the need for learning the English language.

2. Color differences have not allowed people to blend as quickly with the dominant race. Feelings against "mixed" marriage between young people of different colors have hindered their meeting. This is in direct contrast to past generations.

Because of this, nationalism has developed, together with a pride of race and national origin. A swing back to the teaching of culture and language to young people has developed among even some of the European immigrant groups.

Many are now saying, "We do not want to melt. We will not melt." There are now varieties of Americans, each with pride in his national origin. Black Americans and Native Americans have provided the inspiration for Asian Americans, Cuban Americans, Mexican Americans, and so on. Each would indicate they were born here, claim American citizenship, but retain ties to their own country from which their forefathers immigrated. Added to this is the new influx of immigrants who find their identity with their own cultural group.

These ethnic groupings will not quickly lose their identity, since their numbers are constantly growing from the home nation. The "melting" theory is not reasonable for today. There is a better way to explain the United States of today. We have the new terms "stew pot" and "mosaic," indicating some blending of flavor but retaining many qualities of the original ingredient. The United States is truly a "nation of nations." Those arriving will adapt to many American ways. But there seems to be little reality in the hope that we will once again have a nation with one unified cultural pattern. The various ethnic groups do not wish to (and probably will not) become one homogeneous unit.

Pluralism

Pluralism is the idea that there is more than one basic substance or principle. Can our nation exist with these varieties of background, color, and value structure? Can the church exist with such variety?

Diversity has been the norm from the beginning of the Christian Church. It was this very question that confronted the Church of Acts. The Council at Jerusalem discussed cultural differences in Acts 15. Peter's advice was well stated: "Now then, why do you try to test God by putting on the necks of the disciples a yoke that neither we nor our fathers have been able to bear? No! We believe it is through the grace of our Lord Jesus that we are saved, just as they are" (Acts 15:10-11, NIV).

It was possible for the Gentiles and the Jews to exist in the same body, to love one another, and still keep their cultural differences, including language. And growth resulted; unity prevailed.

Most cultural groups are not asking for *separation* from the American life-style. Within the church they are not asking for a corner in which they can exist separately from the main body. They do wish, however, a chance to pursue their own cultural values and heritages within the freedom of both the church and the country. They wish to feel a part of the whole—to be accepted as an equal and not as a foreign element.

My education in seminary centered on training to be a missionary. The classes were generally centered on learning how to identify with one given culture in which a missionary might be placed. This worked fine for my family while we were in the Samoan Islands. When we moved to Honolulu, however, we discovered we were in the midst of many races. The church board had a variety of ethnic backgrounds, each with its own thought patterns.

This same dilemma faces many denominations in the United States. They have handled well the missionary situations overseas. They have trained one missionary or a group of missionaries to relate cross-culturally to one particular culture. But now that same sending organization is being faced with many cultural groups in one particular geographical area of the United States. And very little training is available to the leadership in relating to such variety. This type of pluralism can divide the church if proper steps are not taken.

Paternalism

It is easy for the dominant (usually Anglo) culture to develop a spirit of paternalism, an idea of "lording over" minority groups as a protective father or mother might do to their children.

Differences exist in the church life of various ethnic groups. Although we use the same Bible, feel the same Spirit, practice the same evangelistic zeal, the worship style and practices may vary greatly. Length of services, method of evangelism, tempo and interpretation of hymns, order of worship, and other typical items may vary, but the spirit remains the same.

The dominant group could easily adopt the feeling that "they" must be just like "us." If the ethnic minority church is receiving financial aid, there might prevail an attitude that they really do not have a choice about adapting.

It is possible for the "parent" church to allow the "baby" church to develop its own culture, with its own personality, without surrendering the essentials of the gospel. Within ethnic minority groups, diversity should be encouraged. Identification with, and knowledge of, the culture of the people will greatly aid in the evangelization of the residents from that culture and the new immigrants as they arrive.

The ability of a church to adapt to the needs of a changing community is a strength, not a weakness. Failure to adapt will no doubt mean a failure to meet the needs of a particular culture. It will mean losing a chance to evangelize a community.

Unity

It takes only a few scriptures to convince an open mind that unity is a primary principle of the Bible.

> So in Christ we who are many form one body, and each member belongs to all the others (Rom. 12:5, NIV).

34

There is neither Jew nor Greek, slave nor free, male nor female, for you are all one in Christ Jesus (*Gal. 3:28, NIV;* see also 1 Cor. 10:17 and Eph. 4:13).

I appeal to you, brothers, in the name of our Lord Jesus Christ, that all of you agree with one another so that there may be no divisions among you and that you may be perfectly united in mind and thought *(1 Cor. 1:10, NIV;* see also 2 Cor. 13:11; Eph. 4:3; Phil. 1:27; and 1 Pet. 3:8).

Unity does not mean *uniformity.* We are to be one in spirit and truth. Uniformity means the same in every respect. It implies a lack of diversity or variation. It is difficult to find that in one family, let alone in one church. It is foolish for any culture to impose its ideals and principles on another, no matter in what country one might be.

There are thousands of communities where redemption is not open to all people because persons must conform in order to belong. They must have the same language, enjoy the same worship styles, accept the caste system according to the color of their skin, and adjust to the socioeconomic ladder for leadership. They do not reject the Savior, but in such a situation they simply cannot feel comfortable in the church in which they are not accepted.

Unity means accepting others just as they are. It means allowing for differences, adjusting to those that may be offensive to our culture, and loving each other amid the diversity.

The Church of Jesus Christ can have congregations of various languages and cultures and still feel the spirit of unity. One church facility can house several language groups and not lose the feeling of oneness possible through His love.

What is encouraged here is not segregation. All people should be free to worship in whatever congregation they feel comfortable. To the contrary, no one should be forced to worship in a congregation in which he is uncomfortable because of language or culture. All should be offered choice, so that all might be free to bring their friends to receive what they have received.

WHERE ARE THE FIELDS?

Where are the Hispanics? Would you name Colorado or Arizona as one of the top states? Maybe. But demographics show Minnesota as having a higher percentage of Hispanics than either of these states. The Church of the Nazarene recently sent summer ministry teams of college-age young people to Iowa to start two new Spanish-speaking churches. Who would have picked Muscatine or Marengo, Iowa, as church-planting possibilities for Hispanics?

Where are the Southeast Asians? You might not choose Albuquerque, N.Mex.; Richmond, Va.; Kansas City; or Rochester, Minn. But in all of these cities thriving evangelistic missions are taking place among Cambodians. Thirty-four percent of all Vietnamese live in California, but a recent *National Geographic* article featured 1,300 Vietnamese families who are now in Biloxi, Miss. Nashville is the site of a Buddhist temple especially catering to Southeast Asians.

In the Appendix there are 12 charts illustrating ethnic population clusters in the United States. (Statistics are taken from the 1980 census.) These will help locate the mission fields here in our land.

PRAYER IS THE KEY

Ask the Lord of the harvest, therefore, to send out workers into his harvest field. Go! *(Luke 10:2-3, NIV).*

Spiritual preparation must have the highest priority over all other items. There is no substitute for time spent alone with God. He wants to prepare us properly by:

1. Teaching us to abandon any worldly idols that may weigh us down (1 Sam. 7:3; 2 Chron. 19:3; 2 Cor. 6:16).

2. Cleansing our temple (1 Cor. 3:16; Eph. 2:22; 1 Pet. 2:5).
3. Allowing Him to break up our soil (Hos. 10:12).
4. Making us ready to receive personal purification (1 Thess. 5:23-24; 2 Tim. 2:21; Heb. 10:10; James 4:8).

It will help to combine scripture study in your prayer time. Passages such as Matt. 9:35-38; 25:14-30; 28:19-20; Mark 4:1-20; John 4:27-35; 20:19-30; Rom. 12:1-8; 1 Cor. 12:12-27; Eph. 1:18-23; 4:1-16; and 2 Pet. 3:1-12 would be helpful in guiding your prayers.

Be specific in your prayers. Make a list and do not be afraid to share it with others who might share your concern for evangelizing the nearby ethnic community.

We must not minimize the fact that we are in spiritual warfare with the devil. If we do not receive miracles from God we cannot expect to succeed.

Our responsibilities are to:
1. Trust God for a miracle (1 Cor. 3:6).
2. Yield ourselves to Him personally (Rom. 12:1).
3. Consecrate all our resources to Him—including our minds (Ps. 32:8).

You can be an effective instrument of the Holy Spirit in reaping the harvest, which God's Word declares to be both plentiful and ripe.

3

Barriers to Cross-cultural Evangelism in American Culture

Little systematic attention has been given to the effects of cultural values on cross-cultural communication in the United States. Assumptions, values, and patterns must be considered when properly communicating with the neighbor next door. Certainly these are needed considerations when thinking of ministering to a cultural block close to your church.

The responsibility for cultural adjustment must be shared by both the resident or dominant culture and the incoming or minority culture. In most cases in the United States, the Anglo culture is the resident or dominant culture. Because of immigration facts already discussed, we have unfortunately developed a melting philosophy. As many writers point out, for the first 180 years of U.S. history most incoming cultures quickly melted into the traditional ways. Admittedly, they brought some of their customs and some of these were adopted. Overall, however, the newcomer was expected to learn the English language and blend in culturally as quickly as possible. It is a common perception that the incoming or minority culture must do all the adjusting.

In recent years, many newcomers have brought their own language and ways with a determination to keep them alive. This, coupled with the American Black and Native American distinctives, has set up some real barriers between cultures.

Assuming the Anglo-American has definite responsibilities as the dominant or resident culture, we must examine some cultural distinctives that might cause barriers between them and other cultures. In no way can we presume to cover these thoroughly or solve the complex problems that exist because of these obstacles. But it is important that we look at and allow our minds to begin to think on some of these cultural walls.

LANGUAGE

1. Word Usage

Language affects the way we live. The words we use and the way we use them are, in part, a description of our very lives. One can listen to a person speaking and many times locate his country of origin by the words he uses. It is, therefore, easy for a lifelong resident of the United States to misunderstand another American completely because of a difference in the definition of the words used.

2. Perception

With the eyes able to distinguish 7.5 million colors and the ear approximately 340,000 tones, it is no wonder that language is influenced by a culture's perception. Smell, touch, taste, and the other senses contribute to a richness of experience that lies beyond imagination.

The Eskimo, for example, has 86 different words for "snow." He would obviously be more aware of the subtle variations of that phenomenon than we, as indicated by our one word. (The Samoans have no word for snow, except one adapted from the English.) Likewise, a culture that has no words to describe religious experiences will have far more difficulty understanding Christianity than one rich with religious training. People working with a culture void of Christian background would need to disciple new converts in a simple manner. Biblical references and cliches would be meaningless at the start of discipleship and should be taught carefully. On the other hand, a culture rich with religious and Christian training would quickly understand and could be discipled more rapidly.

VALUES

Our culture has assigned values to different activities. One has come a long way in understanding other cultures when he realizes our values may be different and not always correct.

1. Degrees of Sin

Most cultures have a tendency to assign worse punishment for some wrongs than for others. While the worst sin in our judicial system may be murder, in another culture it might be stealing from one's relatives. You can see how this would affect behavior and thought patterns. A pastor in the United States might be removed immediately for adultery but hardly frowned on for cheating on his Sunday School statistics. In another culture adultery may not be treated quite as harshly. When confronting a culture with values different from one's own, it is best to treat sin as sin. A new look at the sermons of Jesus will give a lesson on confronting sin cross-culturally. When, however, we decide to really treat sin as sin, it is best to remember that what is good for the student is good for the teacher.

2. Obsession with Buildings

Many evangelical churches were founded on ministering to the needs of the poor. The original *Manual of the*

Church of the Nazarene defines the "field of labor" as the "neglected quarters of the city." Dr. Bresee, founder of said church, stated: "We want places so plain that every board will say welcome to the poorest. . . . Let the Church of the Nazarene be true to its commission; not great and elegant buildings; but to feed the hungry and clothe the naked, and wipe away the tears of sorrowing; and gather jewels for His diadem."

However, the Church of the Nazarene and other denominations in the United States have conformed to the pattern of the culture in which they exist. The cultural values of Americans have crept into the church. Detrimental aspects of this value system have been:

a. Each individual congregation has claimed ownership of the property entrusted to them. Without proper teaching, this possessiveness can lead to selfishness when some other cultural or language group wishes to share the facility. Proper teaching will show that all possessions, including church property, belong to God and are to be used in any way necessary to win the neighborhood in which they are found.

b. Another negative effect of American cultural values is that buildings are constructed for the pleasure of those presently in attendance in the church, with little thought of future outreach. Very little thought is given to the needs of the poor and needy, the immigrants, and the refugees.

c. Since our culture does not smile on several families sharing one house, it is difficult for churches to understand the concept of several churches (or groups of people) using the same facility.

It is important that we recognize in our attempt to communicate cross-culturally that people should take precedence over buildings and that buildings should not be constructed so as to alienate individuals who have a less-than-average standard of living. In every case, growth of a particular con-

41

gregation is greatly inhibited when the major emphasis of a church shifts from people to buildings. This is more so in this age than ever before. The influx of immigrants and refugees has made most neighborhoods multiethnic. Nearly every church must look at reaching beyond the dominant or Anglo culture. Ornate structures will not relate to people of every culture.

3. Materialism

An American almost invariably judges another society by its standards of material welfare, defined in a broad sense as physical comfort and health. The American's acceptance of others will often be based on the work ethic and effective acquisition of things. In contrast, many non-Western cultures will emphasize inner experience, such as character building, more than the accumulation of material wealth. As one American well said: "We make our little girls into beauty queens rather than Madonnas."

Many of the American materialistic values will be rapidly adopted by incoming cultures. However, our mistake is to assume that these values are necessary for acceptance of individuals into our circle of friends.

4. Our Priorities Versus Theirs

The pronoun *I* is capitalized only in English. This may reflect the superior feelings we have in our culture for the individual. This feeling of superiority has helped Americans place their products at the top around the world. However, we have often alienated others by not accepting people for who they are. We feel other people come to the United States so they can be just like us, when probably they come here so they can have the freedom to act and think like themselves.

It is very possible for Americans to border on "cultural communism." We impose on others our values and viewpoints and will not allow them to be a part of the structure unless they fully adjust.

It is to be understood that when cultural values intersect, a form of culture shock will develop. A well-read pastor will be prepared for this and will help guide his flock through it.

Listed at the conclusion of this chapter are some of the basic value conflicts that exist between American and other cultures.

SOCIAL CLASS

The social class of an individual or society is usually judged by wealth, job, and education level. Minorities, unfortunately, ofttimes occupy the lower part of the social order. A cultural stigma develops among such cultures and language groups. These can be real communication barriers. The social status even affects verbal communication. Words used will reflect the socioeconomic level of an individual's existence.

The following chart was compiled by a professor from Michigan State University and Dr. Jon Johnston, professor at Pepperdine University.

Socioeconomic Differences in the Conceptualization of Terms

Term	To a Person in the Middle Class It Means:	To a Person in the Lower Class It Means:
Authority	Security to be taken for granted, wooed (courts, police, etc.)	Something hated, to be avoided
Education	Road to better things for self/children	Obstacle course to be surmounted until kids can go to work
Join a Church	Step necessary for social acceptance	Emotional release
Ideal Goal	To be accepted by the "successful" by accumulating money/property	"Coolness"; to "make out" without attraction of the authorities
Society	The ideal pattern one conforms to in the interests of security/acceptance	The "man"—an enemy to be resisted and suspected

Delinquency	An evil originating outside the middle-class home	One of life's inevitable events; to be ignored unless police get into the act
The Future	A rosy horizon	Nonexistent . . . so live each moment fully
The Street	A pathway for cars	A meeting place, providing an escape from a crowded home
Liquor	Sociability/cocktail parties	A means to welcome oblivion
Sex	An adventure and binding force for the family; creates problems of birth control	One of life's few free pleasures
Money	A resource to stretch for daily needs and save for the future	Something to be used now before it disappears
Father	Protector, provider, pal, like God is	Someone hardly ever home who beats mother, drinks, and gambles
Television	One of the many home entertainment devices; preferred less than reading	Illusionary doorway to inaccessible things, places, and people of the world
Welfare	A foolish means of giving money to the lazy and taking it from the hard-working; supports illegitimacy	Survival; the only fair way to distribute resources of society; step toward an eventual "guaranteed income"

More of these terms related to religious values will be included in the next chapter.

The evangelical church as a whole has largely lived up to John Wesley's prediction for Methodism. He prophesied that lower-class Methodists would elevate themselves in social class with each generation. We have, therefore, lost touch with the lower strata of our society and largely with the minorities. Upward mobility is our undoing, unless specific plans are made to reach back to the poor and needy.

PACE AND MOTIVATION

Few cultures live at the daily fast pace of the United States. So much of our opinion of others is based on their ability to be busy and on time. Lack of productivity is often overlooked in favor of a busy schedule. Those cultures that are highly motivated to an active life-style are accepted more readily by Americans.

Forms of Government

Democracy has treated us well. It is a form of government for which most of us would fight. Because of this, it is easy for Americans to equate democracy and the American government with the "biblical way." People who have existed under more repressive forms of government might not immediately understand our way of government. Assuredly it is difficult for some people to catch on to voting, lobbying, registration, taxes, and other government regulations and privileges. This confusion carries over into the church also, since most United States denominations base their governmental structure on the democratic way. (This will be discussed further in the next chapter.)

It is important that new cultures migrating into the United States learn to live with our governmental structure. Americans need to exercise patience and feel personal responsibility to aid in the adjustment of these new residents.

Anticity Bias

There are more than 1,400 references in both Testaments to cities. These references describe God's love for, and ministry to, the cities. So many of the references talk about great leaders and taking the message of the gospel to sin-sick cities.

One need only read about Abraham and Lot and their relationship to Sodom, Jonah and his reluctant trip to Nineveh, Joseph and his attempt to save Egypt from starvation, Daniel's ministry to Babylon, Nehemiah and Jerusalem, Barnabas and Antioch, Paul and the Asian churches, and others to realize how much time God spent instructing His messengers about converting the inhabitants of the cities.

However, the Bible itself adds to the bad reputation of the cities. We read in Gen. 4:17 that the first city was built by Cain, a murderer. Babel had its problems, with the people eventually being scattered across the land (11:8). Fire and brimstone was the only alternative for Sodom and Gomorrah because of their sins (19:24).

For centuries writers and speakers of renown have decried the cities. One of our presidents, Thomas Jefferson, once stated that the yellow fever epidemic was beneficial, for it discouraged urban growth.

Our attitude toward the cities may well affect our ability to communicate with cultures that traditionally live there. Most of the ethnic harvest in the United States is in the cities. We must not allow our prejudice against these areas to slow our evangelistic thrust among other cultures.

GEOGRAPHIC PRIORITIES

At the present time certain geographic areas of the United States hold more potential for ethnic harvest than others. Several factors enter into this:

1. The Migration Patterns of Ethnic People

Initial and secondary migration of ethnic population groups are based mainly on family and climate. There is, therefore, a tendency for some areas of the country to have larger populations of a particular group than others.

2. The Geographic Location

The borders of our country seem to attract a large flow of newcomers. However, in recent years it has become more and more difficult to find an area of the United States not touched by the influx of immigrants and refugees.

3. The Attitude of the Resident or Dominant Culture

Churches and businesses might be more ready to accept new residents from outside our country in some geographic areas than in others. This attitude will determine whether a church would want to share facilities or help an ethnic congregation find their own building.

LACK OF RACIAL UNDERSTANDING

A large number of Americans cannot correctly define the term *race*. Surveys have shown, for instance, that a significant number believe Jews are a race. Others, despite significant education to the contrary, still state they would hesitate accepting a blood donation from someone who is not their skin color.

It is surprising how many, even in the church, view prejudice as an acceptable fact of life.

Misinformation can only create division and misunderstanding. Myths like those stated above must be replaced with proper teaching. We can talk about love and acceptance in the church, but we also are obligated to have a head full of correct information.

This chapter does not suggest American values and cultural patterns are wrong. However, an attempt has been made to show a few of the stumbling blocks that must be avoided if we are to be well informed.

Summary of
Conflicting Cultural Assumptions and Values*

American	Contrast-American

1. Definition of Activity

a. How do people approach activity?
   (1) Concern with doing, progress, change — Being
      External achievement — Spontaneous expressions
   (2) Optimistic, striving — Fatalistic

b. What is the desirable pace of life?
   (1) Fast, busy — Steady, rhythmic
   (2) Driving — Noncompulsive

c. How important are goals in planning?
   (1) Stresses means, procedures, techniques — Stresses final goals

d. What are important goals in life?
   (1) Material goals — Spiritual goals
   (2) Comfort and absence of pain — Fullness of pleasure and pain
   (3) Activity — Experience

e. Where does responsibility for decisions lie?
   (1) Each individual — Function of a group or resides in a role

f. At what level do people live?
   (1) Operational, goals evaluated in terms of consequence — Experimental truth

g. On what basis do people evaluate?
   (1) Utility (does it work?) — Essence (ideal)

h. Who should make decisions?
   (1) The people affected — Those with proper authority

American	Contrast-American
i. What is the nature of problem solving?	
(1) Planning behavior	Coping behavior
(2) Anticipates consequences	Classifies the situation
j. What is the nature of learning?	
(1) Learner is active (student-centered learning)	Learner is passive (serial, rote learning)

2. Definition of Social Relations

American	Contrast-American
a. How are roles defined?	
Attained	Ascribed
Loosely	Tightly
Generally	Specifically
b. How do people relate to others whose status is different?	
(1) Stresses equality	Stresses hierarchical ranks
Minimizes differences	Stresses differences, especially to superiors
(2) Stresses informality and spontaneity	Stresses formality; behavior more easily anticipated
c. How are sex roles defined?	
Similar, overlapping	Distinct
Sex equality	Male superiority
Friends of both sexes	Friends of same sex only
Less legitimized	Legitimized
d. What are members' rights and duties in a group?	
(1) Assumes limited liability	Assumes unlimited liability
(2) Joins group to seek own goals	Accepts constraint by group
(3) Active members can influence group	Leader runs group, members do not.
e. How do people judge others?	
(1) Specific abilities or interests	Overall individuality of person and his status

American	Contrast-American
(2) Task-centered	Person-centered
(3) Fragmentary involvement	Total involvement
f. What is the meaning of friendship?	
(1) Social friendship (short commitment, friends shared)	Intense friendship (long commitment, friends are exclusive)
g. What is the nature of social reciprocity?	
(1) Real only	Ideal and real
(2) Nonbinding (Dutch treat)	Binding
(3) Equal (Dutch treat)	Unequal
h. How do people regard friendly aggression in social interaction?	
(1) Acceptable, interesting, fun	Not acceptable, embarrassing

3. Motivation

American	Contrast-American
a. What is motivating force?	
(1) Achievement	Ascription
b. How is person-person competition evaluated?	
(1) As constructive, healthy	As destructive, antisocial

4. Perception of the World (World View)

American	Contrast-American
a. What is the (natural) world like?	
(1) Physical	Spiritual
(2) Mechanical	Organic
(3) Use of machines	Disuse of machines
b. How does the world operate?	
(1) In a rational, learnable, controllable manner	In a mystically ordered, spiritually conceivable manner (fate)
(2) Chance and probability	No chance or probability
c. What is the nature of man?	
(1) Apart from nature or from any hierarchy	Part of nature or of some hierarchy

50

American	Contrast-American
(2) Impermanent, not fixed, changeable	Permanent, fixed, not changeable
d. What is the relationship between man and nature?	
(1) Good is unlimited.	Good is limited.
(2) Man should modify nature for his ends.	Man should accept the natural order.
(3) Good health and material comforts are expected and desired.	Some disease and material misery are natural, to be expected.
e. What is the nature of truth? goodness?	
(1) Tentative (working type)	Definite
(2) Relative to circumstances	Absolute
(3) Experience analyzed in separate components; dichotomies	Experience apprehended as a whole
f. How is time defined? Valued?	
(1) Future (anticipated)	Past (remembrance) or present experience
(2) Precise units	Undifferentiated
(3) Limited resource	Not limited (not resource)
(4) Lineal	Circular, undifferentiated
g. What is the nature of property?	
(1) Private ownership important as extension of self	Use for "natural" purpose regardless of ownership

5. Perception of the Self and the Individual

American	Contrast-American
a. In what sort of terms is self defined?	
(1) Diffuse, changing terms	Fixed, clearly defined terms
(2) Flexible behavior	Person is located in a social system

American	Contrast-American
b. Where does a person's identity seem to be?	
(1) Within the self (achievement)	Outside the self in roles, groups, family, clan, caste, society
c. Nature of the individual	
(1) Separate aspects (intent, thought, act, biographical background)	Totality of person
d. On whom should a person place reliance?	
(1) Self	Status, superiors, patron, others
(2) Impersonal organizations	Persons
e. What kind of person is valued and respected?	
(1) Youthful (vigorous)	Aged (wise, experienced)
f. What is the basis of social control?	
(1) Persuasion, appeal to the individual	Formal, authoritative
(2) Guilt	Shame

---

*David S. Hoopes and Paul Ventura, eds., *Intercultural Source Book* (Chicago: Intercultural Press, 1979), 48-51.

4

Barriers to Cross-cultural Evangelism in Evangelical Culture

In addition to barriers distinctive to the American culture, there are a few bolstered by Christians and especially the evangelical world. This may begin a process of thinking in the reader's mind that will spur creative solutions to these and other barriers that are recognized.

THE POOR AND FREEDOM FROM SIN

"Redemption and lift" is the theory that people who are saved from their sins will naturally lift themselves socio-economically. The time factor may vary, but seldom does the principle change. One of the possible negative offshoots of this theory is a feeling that sin and poverty are concomitant.

When middle- and upper-class Christians, including evangelical Christians, talk of their comparative wealth in terms of God's blessing, they imply that their good fortune is an evidence of God's favor, the result of their righteousness. At the same time they also imply that the poverty of the poor is an evidence of God's displeasure, the result of their unrigh-

teousness. While this view does not arise from Christian be-
lief, it appears to be commonly practiced in everyday conversation and life.

Ethnic people in the United States are not all poor. However, it is generally accepted that a higher percentage of ethnics are poor, and their per capita income is far below whites.

SOCIAL CONCERN AND LIBERALISM

Denominations vary in their origins. Dr. Timothy L.
Smith writes in his book *Revivalism and Social Reform* about
the holiness movement of the late 19th and early 20th centuries. He documents, from early writings, that many denominations can trace their beginnings to both social reform and
social ministries. In contrast to their history, however, most
holiness denominations today are fearful of social action because of its liberalizing effect on mainline denominations.
Somehow churches today must be able to distinguish between political activism and compassion for the needs of the
less fortunate.

Paul, in his much-quoted admonition in his first letter to
the Thessalonians (5:23-24), calls for the blameless preserva-
tion of the spirit and soul and body. What more is there to
preserve? The teachings of Jesus and Paul would support a
holistic ministry that ministers to the body, as well as the soul
and spirit.

PREJUDICE AND SIN

Prejudice is defined by *The Random House Dictionary* as
"an unfavorable opinion or feeling formed beforehand or
without knowledge, thought, or reason." Mendell Taylor calls
it "weighing the facts with your thumb on the scales." Prejudice is usually followed by discrimination, or acts intended to
harm, injure, or suppress another person.

Preachers have been known to use the pulpit for sermonizing extreme views ranging from acceptance of racial inequality to the complete eradication of prejudice when one is filled with the Holy Spirit. The truth must lie somewhere between these extremes.

Sociologist Rokeach declared: "My research reveals that the more conservative one's theology is, the more bigoted and prejudiced one is likely to be." What a startling statement! Gordon Allport's research discovered that this is only true for what he termed "extrinsic" conservative church people. He defines these as "more interested in religious comfort than religious challenge; getting rather than giving; rules rather than people; and outward appearance rather than inward condition." He points to "intrinsic" conservative Christians as those who manifest interest in challenges, giving, people, and inward condition. Allport further points out that intrinsic conservative Christians tend to be far less prejudiced.

Ministers must teach that God does make a difference in our lives when we are converted. The Holy Spirit at work in us can permeate to the deepest attitudinal levels. However, we must realize that prejudice (though built on sinful attitudes) is taught largely by culture.

In a recent meeting between Cambodians and Vietnamese in Cleveland, it was pointed out that the children of these two national heritages refused to ride in a van together. One leader of the Vietnamese stated that maybe it would help to sit down with the children and explain that this is not proper. How, one might ask, could these leaders take out of these children something the parents had been teaching for years? When you see extreme prejudice in a child you can usually see similar attitudes in the parents.

Prejudice is therefore best dealt with in the careful discipling of sanctified hearts, manifesting interest in challenges, giving, people, and inward condition, rather than comfort, getting, rules, and outward appearance. Prejudice can be conquered in the heart with a combination of God's grace and careful instruction.

WORSHIP AND STUDY FORMS

It is impossible to detail the wide variety of worship and study forms in this short space. We must realize that culture and socioeconomics play a large part in the way one wishes to worship and the manner in which one studies the Bible. It is rather idealistic to think we can develop worship forms, hymnbooks, Sunday School lessons, marriage ceremonies, and rituals that will communicate in other languages and cultures by simply translating them.

A pastor said to me, "I can go anywhere in the United States and know the songs, study the same lesson series, and worship just like I can at home." Maybe that is why his denomination is more successful in one geographic area than another. We must adjust our worship style geographically and culturally if we expect to reach all people with the Christian message. The same principles we have used for years overseas must now be used throughout the United States. The churches of today meet in many languages among various distinguishable cultures in the United States alone. Each has its own style of worship and study. The more we squeeze them into the American mold, the slower they grow.

WE ARE THE TELLERS—THEY ARE THE LISTENERS

Christian missions has ofttimes been based on a white, Anglo teller and a nonwhite listener. In most cases the fields that have allowed indigenous leaders to develop have seen the most rapid growth. At home it is a little harder to surrender control. However, the Christian message is best expressed to Chinese by a Spirit-filled Chinese minister. And a Spanish-speaking church in San Antonio can best be administered by a Spirit-filled Hispanic leader. White-Anglo domination of leadership in any denomination will drive ethnics into developing their own denominations or turn them off to the Christian message completely.

BUILDINGS ARE ESSENTIAL TO GROWTH

Building centeredness was covered in the last chapter. We have developed a "theology of place" that is not always healthy. There is something to be said for the need of identity in a certain place by a group, somewhere to bring family and friends, an identified place for corporate worship.

But there must also be a recognition of financial facts. In thinking of the ethnic influx into the United States and the diversity of cultures this represents, it is mind-boggling to try to conceive of providing buildings for every separate culture in each location where it is needed.

A recent survey in the Church of the Nazarene discovered that a full 20 percent of the churches in the United States were located in counties where 10,000 or more Spanish-speaking people were resident. In these same counties there were no Spanish-speaking Nazarene churches. If they were to try to build 1,000 new buildings for these locations, the cost would be beyond reach.

Several denominational decisions should be considered when finding churches in similar situations. I would suggest the following:

1. It is possible for several language groups to share facilities. In some cases they may want to share ownership and upkeep of the one property.

2. Churches in heavy ethnic population areas or potential concentrations or transition should design buildings for multiple services and multiple use. Architects can show how present buildings could be remodeled to facilitate multiple use.

3. Pastors and district leaders must be acquainted with the needs and potential of using our buildings as often as possible.

As mentioned earlier, we are taught to have only one family in each house. Therefore, we have difficulty thinking of more than one church family being resident in one church building. If the needs of the present United States population are to be met, we have no choice but to change our previous thought pattern.

ENGLISH IS ESSENTIAL TO LEADERSHIP

A report surfaced regarding one denomination's licensing committee who refused to ordain a candidate because he had not passed the proper English course required in the United States. We must guard against telling God He can only call English-speaking men and women to minister in America. Whether we like it or not, it is possible to be born and die in the United States and never speak English. It is also possible to minister in many areas of the United States and not know English.

The English language, however, is certainly necessary for those who plan to make this their home. Denominational leadership must develop methods to help non-English-speaking people become functional in America. We must also recognize those whose English abilities are limited. We will suggest solutions for this dilemma in a later chapter.

DEMOCRACY AND SPIRITUALITY

Missionaries have for years had to learn to bridle their tongues when living in nondemocratic countries. They have believed so strongly in democracy that they were almost willing to jeopardize their ability to spread the gospel in order to speak out for freedom of the individual.

Although democracy is an excellent form of government and does develop more freedom for various religious activities, it also tends to slow down church growth. Some countries under communism and dictatorial governments have shown very rapid growth, while denominations among the middle and upper classes in Western countries are showing slow growth or rapid decline.

We would not want to call for mass persecution or encourage repressive governments of course, but we should recognize that ethnics are most reachable as they come out of persecution. As they adjust to the U.S. life-style, their receptivity to the gospel many times declines.

CLEANLINESS AND GODLINESS

Some of the most often quoted so-called scriptures do not even exist in the Bible. One of these is quoted by Wesley: "Cleanliness is, indeed, next to godliness." With the church's emphasis on holy living and application of scriptures like "clean hands, and a pure heart" (Ps. 24:4), the American interpretation of cleanliness has been firmly planted in people's minds. Very few cultures share our unusual desire for everything to be clean. We will drop perfectly clean food on a freshly scrubbed floor and declare it dirty. We ofttimes confuse dirty with messy. It is possible to overemphasize external cleanliness and thereby bring a misinterpretation of internal purity.

TIME VALUE AND SPIRITUALITY

When my family arrived in Samoa, we discovered that Sunday School was to start at 8 A.M. and morning worship at 9 A.M. But Sunday School rarely started before 9 A.M., and worship somewhere around 10 A.M.

In our family we learned from birth that church is not quite as good if it does not start on time. Samoans had no such concept. We finally decided to make a public announcements: "We are starting on time next Sunday if we are the only ones here." Sure enough, we were the only ones there—and we did not start. The next Sunday we scheduled services differently. Sunday School would be at 9 A.M. and worship at 10 A.M. However, we just did not tell the Samoans. They came when they were ready, and I felt like they were coming closer to being "on time."

Actually, the starting or ending time has nothing to do with the spirituality of the church. It is important that the culture's time value be considered in planning services. This is especially true if one facility is being shared by several cultural groups. Special caution must be observed here so this barrier does not trip up efforts to communicate cross-culturally.

RESPONSIBILITY FOR ONE'S ACTIONS

In a culture where family or clan leaders dictate the needs and wishes of the individual, responsibility for personal actions are often passed on to the leaders. Maturity may come slower in such cultures. Therefore, understanding personal responsibility toward sin may develop later in life. Certainly patience and understanding are necessary when a decision for salvation is faced. Discipleship is impossible without a correct understanding of the culture with which you are working.

Barriers are not always stumbling blocks. If understood and used they can be hurdles that define progress. They must not be allowed to keep us from the unity of the Spirit that is possible through Jesus Christ.

Socioeconomic Differences in the Conceptualization of Terminology Related to Religion

Term	To a Person in the Middle Class It Means:	To a Person in the Lower Class It Means:
Christian, Salvation	A means whereby one organizes and disciplines life	An emotional release (catharsis) that explains one's plight
Mothers' Day	Sunday in May when moms are honored with gifts and loving attention	The first of the month when women receive their welfare check
Job	Means of making/saving money and obtaining status	Way to make bucks to survive; place to go to keep welfare people off your back
College	Means of mind expansion and obtaining "union card" to enter societal circles	Where rich, smart, and lucky go; its information is unrelated to real life
Marriage	Proper institution to raise family and legitimatize sex	Way to solve illegitimacy and/or escape a crowded home
Crime	Intolerable	Part of everyday existence; a way to equalize society's goods
Friend	Mutual identification and acceptance	Someone to hang out with, who experiences your misery
Leisure Time	Time to relax or go on a vacation; welcomed	Time when you cannot make money and lack money to go on a vacation; creates dreaded boredom
The Past	A fascinating adventure to think about; roots to full appreciation of the present	More painful than the present; not to be thought about with pride
Food	A necessity for social, as well as physical, survival; taken for granted	A greatly appreciated and little-diagnosed commodity; not taken for granted
Fine Arts	Something to learn to appreciate so one can appear to have class	Something only upper classes appreciate; a waste of money
Public Park	Place for family recreational activity	Place where kids hang out to promote gangs
Hooker/ Prostitute	Disgusting, dirty woman who traps innocent men	Lady making money and performing a needed service for uptight higher-class males

5

Developing a Plan

God has always worked from a well-developed plan. The creation itself was in an orderly sequence. Man was created only after a proper environment existed. Jesus also emphasized good planning.

> Suppose one of you wants to build a tower. Will he not first sit down and estimate the cost to see if he has enough money to complete it? For if he lays the foundation and is not able to finish it, everyone who sees it will ridicule him, saying, "This fellow began to build and was not able to finish" *(Luke 14:28-30, NIV).*

Good planning will eventually produce plans that are reasonable to carry out. Elaborate plans beyond the ability of those involved will only occupy space in some church storage area. Each plan must include action to be taken, deadlines, assignments, and a method of evaluation.

The following six steps are designed to help in the process of getting ready to plant a cross-cultural work. They are listed briefly here, then expanded below.

Step 1—*Let's Get Started*
Someone must be the spark—that one who takes the initiative. Some beginning inquiry to test the feelings of others is necessary from the start.

Step 2—*Are There Others?*

It is important that enough personnel be recruited to make the effort work. A small group called a Mission Action Committee (M.A.C.) should be formed.

Step 3—*Not Too Fast*

Because everyone is busy, it is essential to take the proper time to raise the awareness of the sponsoring group or groups. It is important to create in the minds and hearts of the members of the group a sensitivity toward people who are "different from us."

Step 4—*A Satellite View*

The M.A.C. must be able to get an overall view and gather the facts necessary to make reasonable decisions. It is important to begin by arriving at a purpose statement. Then, a proper study of the community will be conducted. Needs will be prioritized, goals set, and an action plan developed. If all this makes your head swim, hold on; there are more resources coming that will aid in your journey.

Step 5—*What Does All This Mean?*

The materials collected are now ready to be evaluated. These final times together as a Mission Action Committee are very important. By the time you arrive at this step you are very close to arriving at your dream—a new baby church. Do not rush past this opportunity to sit down in a retreat setting and talk about everything.

Step 6—*Let's Go to Work*

Implementation now is possible. We will briefly review some examples of churches that have succeeded in their effort to plant a church cross-culturally in chapter 6.

The time needed for your church to go through this process will depend on many factors: the size of the church and the scope of the survey areas selected, how complete your work is, and the priority given to this project by its leaders. The following time line will help you gauge your progress:

Step 1	1-2 weeks
Step 2	2-4 weeks
Step 3	2-4 weeks
Step 4	4-12 weeks
Step 5	1-3 weeks
Step 6	3-5 weeks
	13-30 weeks

STEP 1: LET'S GET STARTED

There are two directions a church can take:

1. Drifting

I grew up in a church in the 40s and 50s that had the same ethnic and socioeconomic profile as its neighborhood. Today that church has relocated because of the changing neighborhood. In another church I attended, people asserted, "Basically the program of our church today is what it was 30 years ago." In both churches, the spiritual needs are not being met, and the attendance figures are declining every year. They are what one might call "drifting" churches. There is no sense of direction and no sense of mission for those in their area to whom they cannot minister because of language or cultural differences.

You can be the one to initiate change. Whether you are a pastor or layman, you can be the spark that will light the flame of evangelism to a new ethnic group to whom your church is not now ministering.

2. Directional

Directional is the opposite of drifting. The directional church is one in which the pastor, leadership, and laity cooperate, get all the facts, and then make a responsible decision about the future course to take. It may lead to a non-English

Sunday School class. Your church building may be used by several non-English-language congregations. There might be a need in an adjoining community where an ethnic outreach is needed. You might even initiate a cooperative effort between you and a nearby church.

Someone must begin. It does not matter who is the first to suggest, "Let's go." Do it; be that one.

STEP 2: ARE THERE OTHERS?

Each effort to minister among the ethnic groups of the United States should be supported by a Mission Action Committee. This is simply a committee of interested people who are willing to put time and effort into ministering cross-culturally.

The chairperson of this Mission Action Committee should be an active layperson or the pastor. Those selecting the members of the committee should consider the following guidelines:

1. They should have a strong commitment to missions.
2. They should exhibit a deep concern for people.
3. They should display experience or a desire to gather, analyze, and develop facts, surveys, and plans.
4. They should relate well to others.
5. They should exhibit leadership skills in their lives.

Make sure personality characteristics are not overlooked. People communicate best cross-culturally if they are adaptable, compassionate, and able to understand and tolerate other people whose ways might be different from theirs.

The committee structure should be flexible and meet the local need. In some cases the program might be led by only the chairperson, who is appointed by the church board. This person would enlist assistance as needed and report directly to the church board and/or pastor.

Where a larger church is involved or where several

churches are cooperating in a missions venture, a committee would be preferred. It is important, however, that this not become burdensome in size. A smaller Mission Action Committee might allow more participation as they delegate duties to subcommittees.

This is only an introduction. A more extensive volume, titled *The Mission Action Sourcebook,* is available through the Nazarene Publishing House, P.O. Box 527, Kansas City, MO 64141.

STEP 3: NOT TOO FAST

Before the Mission Action Committee gets under way, there is some groundwork that must be done. People must be informed of the need, even though the full scope of that need may not be known until further research is finished. The goal should never be to lay guilt on members but to inform and inspire so the harvest might be reaped. Awareness of the presence of people who have a different appearance, language, race, color, or social level will help create understanding by all involved.

The pastor is a key in this area. Sermons on the Samaritan woman or the Good Samaritan are excellent opportunities to communicate the need of reaching cross-culturally in your neighborhood.

Prayer for the leadership of the Holy Spirit is urgently needed. In most cases miracles are needed. Pray that God will miraculously raise the level of interest of Christians so they will cooperate with such a venture. Reaching into ethnics' lives that are surrounded with shallow Christianity or non-Christian background will be difficult. We must have the leadership of the Holy Spirit. Miracles happen when people pray, and they seldom happen when people do not pray. Your committee must commit themselves to daily prayer. Church people must surround you with prayer. Be specific in your requests. Get people to pledge prayer times in their homes, or have small prayer cells focus prayer power on the launching of this new work.

> Again, I tell you that if two of you on earth agree about anything you ask for, it will be done for you by my Father in heaven. For where two or three come together in my name, there am I with them (Matt. 18:19-20, NIV).

> The harvest is plentiful, but the workers are few. Ask the Lord of the harvest, therefore, to send out workers into his harvest field (Luke 10:2, NIV).

Our God is one who leads, directs, and empowers our minds. Jesus knew the disciples would not succeed without the power of Pentecost. They needed it to witness both there in Jerusalem as well as in far-off lands.

There is power available to those who wish to receive it. No committee should head into work of this magnitude without a knowledge that it is led by and filled with the Holy Spirit. Pray for this power before organizing. Pray for it during your sessions. And continue to pray for it as the work progresses.

Special instructions prior to step 4. Make sure those working on this committee are instructed in cultural and cross-cultural relationships. No doubt some help will be received from chapters 3 and 4. Further instructions include the following:

1. God does not put His "Good Culture" seal on any culture. Culture is man-made. No one culture can meet the needs of all people or situations.

2. People have different values, standards of living, approaches to life, and ways of getting things done. Unless this is recognized, hostile feelings and frustrations can easily arise.

3. These differences are not wrong. It is our privilege to do things our way, but others have that right also. This is true in America as well as in other countries.

4. Bridges are best built when similarities are emphasized. Common ground can be found in intercultural relationships.

5. Develop interests in the things that may interest the target ethnic group. Showing genuine concern for knowledge of their homeland, people, religion, government, and everyday life will quickly break down barriers. We can learn to appreciate the positive aspects of all cultures.

6. Learn from other cultures. Their way of doing things may be better than our way.

7. Be ready to be misunderstood. It can and most likely will happen. Many of the aspects of our culture are offensive to other cultures. There are also things in their culture that would be offensive to us. It could be as innocent as a raised eyebrow, a handshake, a greeting, or a lack of attention given at a proper time. While it is important not to go into relationships with fear and trembling, we must remember these times will come. We should not become upset or offended at such misunderstandings.

8. God's Spirit will help us. He wishes all Christians to be one. He, therefore, will guide a willing heart.

9. Learn to communicate in the simplest English possible. You can speak with a small vocabulary without sounding like you are using baby talk.

10. Do not overcompensate. It is natural to try to talk too loud, speak with their accent, or leave out words to try to aid communication with ethnics. Most people learning English understand best when spoken to in a normal voice with correct English spoken distinctly with a limited vocabulary.

11. It is important to remember that you are not sent as a reshaper of another's culture. You are trying to communicate the love of God through your life.

The Home Mission Board of the Southern Baptists gives some general dos and don'ts in cross-cultural communication:

Dos

1. Seek to establish a genuine friendship.

2. See ethnics as individuals and as equals.

3. Learn something of their country, customs, and culture so you may talk intelligently with them and learn more about them. Show appreciation for them.

4. Involve ethnics in wholesome and uplifting activities of all kinds, such as sports events, picnics, sight-seeing trips, musicals, and so on.

5. Take a personal interest in the individual—his background, beliefs, goals, and plans. Respect his beliefs and dietary laws even if you do not have the same.

6. Be yourself. Be sincere, honest, and direct in speech and actions. Use terms the person will understand. Ask for restatement of something you do not understand.

7. Be humble in regard to material and other blessings you, your family, and your country enjoy. Show a spirit of thanksgiving and give tribute to God for His blessings.

8. Share your life, activities, special events, and aspirations with them.

9. Leave subjects open for further discussions.

Don'ts

1. Don't have a condescending attitude.

2. Don't parade your standard of living, country, or accomplishments as being superior.

3. Don't act as though English were the only worthwhile language in the world; rather express regret if you cannot use several languages fluently.

4. Don't ask meaningless questions or those involving cultural or life-style comparisons.

5. Don't show surprise, shock, or hurt feelings at anything an ethnic says or does.

6. Don't generalize or make statements of judgment without really understanding a subject.

7. Don't criticize or argue about people, places, things, politics, or religion.

8. Don't use American slang or idioms without expla-
nation.

9. Don't agree just to be agreeable or when you do not
understand what has been said.

Of primary importance in communicating with ethnics
is to be open, full of concern and love.

STEP 4: A SATELLITE VIEW

The Mission Action Committee is now ready to organize
itself for action. You are not ready to hit the streets yet, however. Some important preliminary work must be done first.

Statement of Purpose

Each situation is unique. Each community has its own
particular needs. We cannot detail in this book each particular situation. It is essential that the committee and key leaders
sit down to decide the real purpose of the outreach to be
attempted.

A statement of purpose is an all-inclusive, understandable, concise, well-defined, and biblically consistent statement of the missionary purpose and direction of the mission
task(s) planned. If the sponsoring church or churches have a
statement of purpose, the committee will want to refer to this
for guidance.

The following questions should be observed:

1. Is the statement *all-inclusive,* covering what needs to
be done in this witness and ministry venture?

2. Is the statement *understandable* to both committee
members and those who are not as involved?

3. Is the statement *concise?* Does it say what it should
say in as brief a manner as possible? Does it come to the
point?

4. Is the statement *well defined?* Does it clearly show
what is planned in the community and the role to be played?

5. Is the statement *consistent with biblical ideals* for church purposes and practices?

If the sponsoring church or churches have no statement of purpose, the M.A.C. might follow these procedures:

1. Invite the pastor(s) and other church leaders to sit with the committee and present their opinions about the missionary responsibilities of the local church at home.

2. The M.A.C. should then enter a brainstorming session, using the ideas presented. Start with God's mission to the world, and slowly narrow it down to the community to be targeted.

3. Final drafting of a purpose statement is better handled by a small subcommittee of two or three.

4. The full M.A.C. will want to review the work of this subcommittee and refine the statement where necessary.

5. It would be best if this statement is presented to the full church board(s) for approval. There might be a desire to expose this to the full congregation.

6. Allow this statement to influence every aspect of your planning. However, do not be afraid to revise or refine the statement as you progress in your work.

Community Study

The committee is now ready to organize itself for a study of the community selected for the site of the cross-cultural work.

There are several reasons why a study of this nature is necessary:

1. To pinpoint the target area to be covered.
2. To understand the present situation in that area.
3. To try to project as accurately as possible the future prospects of the community so as to be able to plan for the future of the church(es) needed.
4. To understand the people who live there, their recep-

tivity to the gospel, their needs, and how best to reach them for Christ.

5. To lay plans based on these facts that will best assure a growing work among the cultural group to be targeted.

Your first question might be, *Where do we look for the information needed?* In most cases the information desired is already available. This is especially true in larger cities. It would be great if there were one place where all this information could be located. Unfortunately, various agencies have various details according to their particular needs. It is important that the committee search out all available information and then compile it for their particular need. Your ingenuity and your willingness to spend time and effort will greatly influence your success. You might check the following sources:

1. Census Information

Facts from a census are probably the most accurate information you can possess because it relies on questions asked of *all* residents in a community instead of a percentage of residents (as in other surveys).

In the U.S., Census Bureau population reports are given by age, sex, ethnic background, education, income, and housing type. All of this information will be broken to census tracts and block divisions. It is possible to chart even the smallest area with this information.

Some sources of U.S. census data are:

  a. Datamap
  9749 Hamilton Rd.
  Eden Prairie, MN 55344
  b. Population Reference Bureau
  1337 Connecticut Ave. N.W.
  Washington, DC 20036
  c. CAPC (Census Access for Planning in the Church)
  Concordia Teachers College
  River Forest, IL 60305

Participating denominations have information that can be processed for any area. For example, in the Church of the Nazarene one would contact:

Mr. Dale Jones
Church of the Nazarene Headquarters
6401 The Paseo
Kansas City, MO 64131

2. County Statistics

A call or a visit to the county offices might turn up some statistics. These might even be more recent than the statistics of the U.S. census. Many clerks in the county offices might not know about these, so do not give up easily. Be willing to go down in person and snoop around.

Check to see if there is a county library which stores county statistics, reports, environmental impact reports, and so on. Talk directly to the librarian. Ask about information and helpful materials that might relate to your assigned area of study.

Talk to the county planning department. They will have information on unincorporated areas that are under county control.

Do not overlook the county supervisors, county superintendent of schools, and any others of which you might think.

3. City Statistics

There might be information available at city hall. Many cities print visitor packets or information for new residents. Likewise, many cities have, for prospective businesses, information packets that include all kinds of information regarding the location of, and trends in, ethnic population movement. If these reports include technical terminology, it is proper to ask questions to help you fully understand the meaning of the facts given.

Many larger cities have information stations at key entry

points. Booklets available there may be published by the city but not available at city hall.

4. School Boards

Most schools are willing to release information on race, age groupings, and geographic locations of their students. They often have studies on projected statistics that might help. If there is a reluctance to share this information, you may have to find a teacher or official in the system who will help you. Since most school boards are elected, however, they are usually happy to supply information to voters just to impress them. This is especially true if they are aware that you are representing a number of voters from that district.

5. Public Utilities

Most utility companies make information available. Many times it is for sale and not distributed free of charge. The utilities regularly sell this information to businesses to help in distribution of product advertisement.

6. Local University Sociology Departments

Many sociology departments require studies of certain areas as classroom assignments for students. These reports are usually up-to-date and accurate. A small fee might be required, but these reports are a great source of information not available at other places.

7. Chambers of Commerce

Most areas keep updating their information to attract businesses and new residents. If they understand your purpose, the information will usually be made available at no cost or only the cost of copying.

8. Television and Radio Stations

It is important to local television and radio stations to keep recent sales and audience statistics. They will usually depend on information from companies such as Arbitron, but may be willing to share information they have.

9. Ethnic Newspapers, Churches, Shops, Restaurants, Clubs, and Theaters

One never knows what information will be available from contacts with ethnic organizations. To overlook them might be to sacrifice that one gem that would lead you to a community need heretofore overlooked.

10. Marketing Companies

Usually marketing companies are expensive sources of information. But their work is extensive so as to provide companies with marketing data that is narrowed to a specific area. Do not buy this blindly. It may not contain what you are looking for.

11. Personal Study

Do not overlook one's individual effort as a necessary item. The particulars of what you want to know about your community probably are not available unless you get out there and drive the streets and knock on doors.

Several helpful personal studies are outlined in the *Mission Action Sourcebook* mentioned earlier. We will note two that should be examined.

A. *Driving and Walking Tour of the Area (Windshield Survey)*

The windshield survey involves several teams. For best results each team should:

• Have a driver and two observers.

• Include one person who has previously lived or presently lives in the community to be surveyed.

Three steps should then be completed:

1. Drive through the community in prescribed blocks. One observer will watch the left while the other looks to the right. All observations will be recorded on paper for further discussion.

2. Take a half-hour walk through the area, making more detailed observations. Talk to people and ask questions.

3. Later that same day sit down with other teams and discuss what you have seen, recording your discussion. Especially try to point out facts learned that will help in planting a new church. Discuss change, and let team members who have lived in the area share the changes they have noticed. Then talk about the impressions those team members have of the community today.

B. *Interviews with Community People (Needs Analysis)*

Interview community leaders who are in touch with people every day. Ask them about the needs of the community and how a new church could help. Include in your interview:

> Public school counselors
> Community mental health directors
> Police agencies
> Social service agency personnel
> Newspaper editors/radio and TV news directors
> Immigration departments
> Housing authorities

You must now ask, *What do we look for in the information we have gathered?* Necessary information will change according to the target people and area. However, generally you are looking for certain uniform elements:

1. Growth Trends

You need to find the numerical and percentage change that is taking place between certain periods of time. For example, you might look at the 1970 figures and compare them with the 1980 statistics. This research of the past and present should, if possible, include some short- and long-range projections.

2. Characteristics of the City/Community

Employment trends, unemployment statistics, the distance people travel to work, traffic patterns and street usage, freeway and main highway arteries, and natural barriers (such as railroads, mountains, freeways, parks, etc.) all will be necessary to know. It is also meaningful to know what areas have certain age, income, social, race, and other characteristics.

3. Characteristics of Target Ethnic Group

Look at family characteristics such as age of head of household, average number of children, marriage patterns, socioeconomic level, and profession. Study the pattern of working wives and female heads of household.

Do not overlook political bias, hobbies, leisure activities, style of homes, dress, personal concerns, needs, and felt needs.

STEP 5: WHAT DOES ALL THIS MEAN?

What is most important? Since the data has been collected, it is time for the Mission Action Committee to meet and decide the priority of the needs and the goals to carry out the plan. If possible, find a secluded place away from the church where concentrated and prayerful consideration can be given to all material. A Friday night through Saturday noon would be the *minimum* time necessary.

The following questions will help in determining the priority of needs:

1. What problems are shared by the majority in the community?
2. Which of the problems most affect the target ethnic group?
3. Are any of these problems being handled adequately by another church or social organization?

4. Considering our resources and personnel, which needs could be best met?

5. Could these needs be met in our facilities or in facilities away from our building?

6. Are our people ready to share our facilities? Is the target group willing to share facilities?

7. Should we start small (such as a language Bible class), or do we have enough contacts to launch a full mission from the beginning?

For the retreat, keep in hand the purpose statement prepared in step 4. The priority-setting and goal-setting sessions might follow these patterns.

1. Have someone read a scripture concerning the harvest of souls (2-3 minutes).

2. Have two or three members lead in prayer, asking the Holy Spirit to guide these final planning sessions (10-15 minutes).

3. Read again the purpose statement (have copies for everyone). Adapt it if necessary, based on the information learned from the surveys and analysis (10-20 minutes).

4. Have copies of all analysis data for each member to review. From this make a list of the community and cultural needs. Write them on a chalkboard or flip chart (15-20 minutes).

5. Isolate a few of these needs (fewer than 10) that are specific in nature. If they are general, large in scope, and hard to define, spend time making them more specific. It might even help first to separate the list into outreach, discipling, social services, administrative, and program (2-3 hours).

6. Make sure each need identified can be met by your group or church. Talk about what might be needed to

accomplish the meeting of each need (10-15 minutes).

7. Develop a goal statement for each priority need. These goals must be specific, attainable, and measurable (1-2 hours).

8. Look at the different types of ethnic churches described in chapter 6. Begin to decide which best meets the needs of the target group and the church.

STEP 6: LET'S GO TO WORK

What needs to be done? Who will do it? When is the deadline? What resources are necessary?

These and other questions are legitimate concerns. Goals, though they be specific, attainable, and measurable, are not automatically put into action.

Subcommittees can be given one goal each to outline and then guided to attainment. It is very important that each goal be set in a timetable. It is better if people assigned to tasks have talents and abilities in that particular area.

Cultivate the Community

A garden must be cultivated before planting. A community is no different. The target people must know about the church long before services begin.

Surveys have shown that 70 percent or more of those who are won to the church are first invited by their friends or relatives. Dr. Win Arn, of the Institute of American Church Growth, gives these findings from 10,000 people questioned:

	%
Those who walk in off the street	3-5
Those who find the church programs attractive and effective	2-3
Those who find the pastor to be the attraction and drawing card	3-6

Those who have special needs	2-3
Those who are won through visitation programs	1-2
Those who are won because of the Sunday School work and emphasis	3-5
Those won in city-wide, interdenominational crusades	.1
Those won by friends and relatives	70-90

Since friendship is so important in winning new people, it is vital that we begin by making friends in the target community. This is especially true among the unsaved. Here are some suggestions:

1. Develop some good printed material that can be distributed in the community. These should be very well designed and preferably in the language of the target ethnic group. In some instances it will be helpful to have bilingual materials. Use this literature to show that your church is aware of their needs and has plans to meet them. Pictures are always useful too.

2. Use the local newspapers. They will usually publicize an organization that wishes to meet the needs of the community. Many times the advertising is free, and often they will even write the articles for you.

3. If finance and personnel are available, use the radio for spot announcements. Some denominations have broadcasts available in a variety of languages.

4. Meet community ethnic leaders and introduce them to any leaders in your church who speak their language.

5. Involve all ages in surveying the neighborhood. If possible, involve people who speak the language of the target area and have been briefed on the local culture. It is possible to use people from a neighboring church if they can help with language difficulties.

6. Look for homes in which to begin Bible studies or classes in English as a second language.

7. Organize the young people of your church in community cleanup projects (if needed).

8. Inside or outside concerts and programs will attract attention to the project. In some areas tent revivals are still being used effectively.

Plan for the Launch

Now that you have surveyed the community, collected the data, and your group is excited, don't hesitate to set a starting date. Study the models in chapters 6 and 7. Don't be afraid to start small. Nothing will stop you—God is on your side!

6

Ethnic Church-planting Models

No two situations are the same. Each neighborhood, language, and church needs its own action plan. Each plan becomes its own model. Several churches, however, have followed somewhat similar patterns. The following criteria have been used to select and describe the models that are used as examples in this chapter.

1. These are actual churches that have been examined by the author.

2. They are successful in that growth and evangelism have taken place. It might be said that the model worked.

3. These models do not seem to have geographic sectional overtones or to have been successful because of their geographic location.

4. Certain adaptations can be made to these models without loss of workability. All the details may not fit any given situation, but the model can still be a usable plan.

These examples are not meant to be exhaustive but illustrative. Other examples no doubt do exist. God-given ingenuity will probably create more in the future.

I. Churches Started
at a Physical Distance from the Sponsor

A. Natural Birth

A church decides to plant an ethnic church in a neighborhood geographically removed from the planting church.

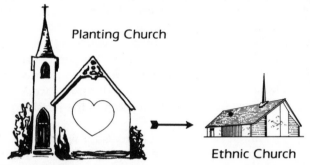

Planting Church

Ethnic Church

1. *Characteristics*
    a. Key laymen and pastoral leaders alike saw spiritual needs in a specific ethnic neighborhood that were not being met.
    b. They were able to transfer this burden to others in the church.
    c. It was impossible to bring the target people to the sponsor's neighborhood on a weekly basis.
        (1) It was physically too far to transport them.
        (2) The socioeconomic differences would have created a barrier.
        (3) The language would have created a wall between the sponsoring church and the ethnic church.
    d. The ethnic neighborhood had a few evangelical churches but none of the sponsor's denomination.
    e. Two ethnic families in the sponsoring church had retained their original language but adopted the Anglo culture.

2. *Positive Ideas from the Model*
   a. The people rightly believed the money they gave for this project was for missions.
   b. They shared their facilities with the baby church for special occasions.
   c. The sponsors were able to loan their building to the ethnic group when the ethnics had important services.
   d. The sponsoring church was able to support the ethnic church for a period of time.
   e. People from the sponsoring church were able to offer advice and support to the mission in fund raising.
   f. Leaders of the sponsoring church used their expertise in long-range planning to help the ethnic work.
   g. The ministers offered fellowship to the mission pastor in the beginning.
   h. The church staff assisted in goals for weaning the mission work from the sponsoring church both in finance and leadership.

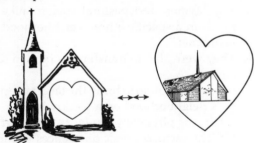

B. Adoption

A sponsoring church finds an existing church in another neighborhood and adopts it to help in its development.

1. *Characteristics*
   a. The ethnic church was at both a physical and a cultural distance from the sponsor.
   b. The mission church needed guidance and help, as they were seeing no growth.

    c. The facilities of the ethnic mission were located in the target neighborhood but were badly in need of repair.

    d. The sponsor church with the trained talent and resources began to feel a burden.

    e. Many persons from the adopted church were new in the United States and did not understand the American business structure. Some business matters like building payments, pastoral support, and so on were confusing to them.

2. *Positive Ideas from the Model*

    a. The sponsoring pastor researched the culture of the ethnic group and learned a few phrases of greeting in their language.

    b. He educated his congregation on the culture of the mission.

    c. He taught his church that they were giving to *missions* in their own city.

    d. Using an interpreter, the sponsoring church trained ethnic Sunday School workers, musicians, and social workers.

    e. On Thanksgiving, the sponsoring members showed their love by reaching out to the extremely needy in the mission group.

    f. The sponsoring church expressed tangible appreciation to the mission pastor at Christmas.

    g. Those with financial expertise gave leadership and training on tithing, budgeting, and a detailed program to help the mission be self-sufficient.

    h. English as a second language was taught, using the Bible as a text.

C. Implantation

A sponsoring church begins an ethnic mission in its buildings, realizing it will eventually need to be transplanted to a neighborhood where it can grow.

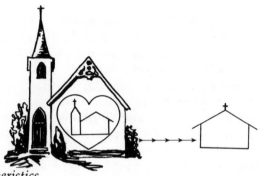

1. *Characteristics*
   a. The sponsoring church had adequate space to begin a new work.
   b. They had available transportation to bring in the ethnic group.
   c. The target ethnic group lived generally in one geographic neighborhood. There was an existing church of the same denomination as the target group in the neighborhood, but several problems existed.
      (1) The existing church was very small.
      (2) The pastor had no cross-cultural experience and could not give the needed help to the target group.
      (3) The existing church could not financially, emotionally, or spiritually support the target mission.
   d. The sponsoring church agreed that when the target group became strong they would be implanted in the existing church.
2. *Positive Ideas from the Model*
   a. The target church began in a positive, supportive atmosphere.
   b. All three churches involved were informed from the beginning of future plans.
   c. The target mission received help from other, uninvolved churches as they relocated to the small existing church.

d. The pastor of the existing church in the target neighborhood gained many insights into cross-cultural church planning by being involved from the beginning.

Introduction to Multicongregational Churches

A recent study conducted by the Church of the Nazarene has resulted in proposed organizational changes to give guidance to several congregations sharing one facility (multicongregations). In the report, the following facts concerning multicongregations in the denomination were revealed:

From its inception, the Church of the Nazarene has recognized the opportunity to minister to these immigrant groups. Dr. Bresee had both Spanish- and Chinese-language works in the original First Church of the Nazarene in Los Angeles. Therefore, the mother church was a multicongregational church.

Today, the most conservative statistics we have indicate there has been tremendous growth in multicongregation churches since 1970. The number of U.S. and Canadian multicongregation churches has grown from 1 in 1976 to 22 in 1980, and to 121 in 1984. This is a 600 percent increase from 1981 to 1984. If this growth pattern continues, it indicates that before 1990 at least 30 percent of our U.S. and Canadian churches will be multicongregational. Of the 450 ethnic works in existence in 1983 (either fully organized churches or church-type missions) nearly 60 percent of them meet in multicongregational church settings.

The reasons for the development of such churches are:

I. The Scriptural Mandate
   A. The fulfillment of the "Great Commission" begins at home (Acts 1:8).
   B. Jesus prayed for the unity of the Church (John 17:20-23).
II. Church Growth Principles
   A. Links the formation of a new congregation to an established church.
   B. Allows for the nurture and development of the new congregation by the "mother" church.

C. Fosters an awareness of "mission" by the established church.
III. Economic Factors
   A. Makes for good stewardship of building and property dollars through the use of facilities by more than one congregation.
   B. Allows the daughter church (ofttimes from a lower income level) to develop without heavy financial strain.
IV. The Immediacy of the Need
   A. People who have recently been uprooted from their cultural setting are most receptive to the gospel message.
   B. To wait until we can reach many of these people groups by traditional means will be too late.

When we see the potential for growth among Blacks, Koreans, Hispanics, Armenians, Filipinos, Chinese, Cambodians, and other ethnic groups, the possibilities for organizing new areas of ministry develop in an astonishing way. We are reminded again of the words of the founder of the Church of the Nazarene, Dr. Phineas F. Bresee, "We are debtors to give the gospel to every creature in the same measure that we have received it."

Two subdivisions of multicongregations will be considered with several models under each.

II. More than One Organized Church Meeting in the Same Building

All congregations work in a continuing fellowship to build unity. All expenses associated with the use of the facilities are shared proportionately by each group. Each group is equally accountable to the district or state church organization.

A. Natural Birth

A church plants another church within its facilities with the intention of keeping it there.

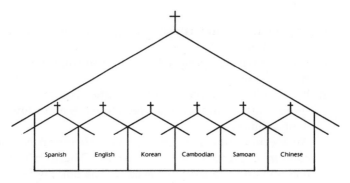

1. *Characteristics*
   a. The English-speaking church was located in a multi-cultural neighborhood.
   b. Through a survey, this church found the community to have five major language groups, including English.
   c. Most of the people preferred to speak their own language and have major social contact within their own culture.
   d. The youth and children spoke the common language, English, as they went to school and social events together. The exceptions to this were preschoolers and recent overseas arrivals.
   e. The cost of land prohibited the purchase of five different church properties.
   f. The mother church had a building that could be converted for multiuse.
2. *Positive Ideas from the Model*
   a. The pastor of the English-speaking church preached once a month for a year on biblical understanding of culture, race relations, love, and cross-cultural evangelism. This took place before any non-English service started.
   b. The planting took place systematically, starting with the largest language group represented in the neighborhood.

c. The financial support was through the mission giving of the church.

d. Each church was pastored by a person from the target ethnic group.

e. Eventually all buildings and properties became the responsibility of all the organized churches according to their abilities.

f. An elected council from each church governed the combined projects of the churches. These included building and property needs as well as Sunday School activities.

g. The five churches hired one youth pastor and one children's minister to pastor to the combined needs, since both age-groups spoke English.

h. Each local church had their own evangelistic thrust, social outreach, and the care of their own church family.

i. The council planned combined services and potluck dinners for cultural awareness once a quarter.

B. Adoption

A church reaches out to an existing church in their neighborhood and adopts them into their church family. They share facilities but exist as two separate organizations.

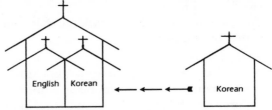

1. *Characteristics*
   a. This was an English-speaking church with facilities larger than they needed.
   b. This congregation was aware it was in a multiracial area.

    c. They were approached by an existing ethnic church in the area who had no place to meet.

    d. The doctrinal stands of both churches were similar.

    e. Facilities could be shared by adjusting the time schedule.

    f. An agreeable financial arrangement made each church able to exist easier than before.

2. *Positive Ideas from the Model*

    a. A new sense of mission was felt by the adopting church as they shared their facilities.

    b. The pastor led his people to the understanding they were assisting in evangelizing a segment of the neighborhood they previously had not been able to reach.

    c. Because of the generosity of the English-speaking church, the ethnic group developed deep respect for them as Americans and for their denomination.

    d. Picnics, combined services, and informal fellowship brought each congregation to a new understanding of the other.

    e. The English church provided a new base for sponsoring immigrants from the ethnic homeland. Many families were united.

    f. English as a second language was taught.

    g. Youth and children's English classes were shared by both congregations since they went to school together.

C. Transition

The neighborhood has changed, and a new church is formed to take over the facility as the existing culture dies out.

Cities grow, evolve, and decline. Sometimes there will be a rebirth and resurrection. Transition is a relative term because it can be slight or a complete change. All of the examples in this chapter are examples of churches in transition.

But in this case complete change has taken place in the community. For the church to continue to exist it has to have a racial as well as a socioeconomic change.

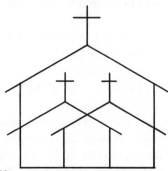

1. *Characteristics*
   a. The neighborhood began racial changes about 12 years ago and had made a 95 percent change.
   b. The church was white, but as Blacks moved in, whites moved to the suburbs.
   c. The church had a small debt, but it was too large for a struggling Black church.
   d. The maintenance and utilities were enormous.
   e. The congregation could not afford a staff.
   f. The church was plagued by vandalism, problems of how to feed the poor, and other social problems.
2. *Positive Ideas from the Model*
   a. An interim pastor was called who was experienced in a changing neighborhood.
   b. Whites and Blacks attended Sunday afternoon discussions on issues involving the change.
   c. Later a Black pastor replaced the interim pastor. He started a service with a free, gospel style. The traditional service of the past continued also.
   d. The new congregation promoted uplift and self-esteem. The Blacks in that neighborhood were told six days a

week they were a minority, but on Sunday they were made to feel important.

e. Solving social problems was linked to evangelistic outreach. The church organized small geographic groups designed to care for each person individually. These care units promoted the idea "Everybody cares for you."

f. Because of the interim situation moving so smoothly, no financial help was needed from outside sources.

III. More than One Culture in One Church Organization

This includes several congregations in one church organization as well as several language classes meeting separately, yet all part of one organization. Each group or class has its own leader. Where possible, ethnic leadership is desirable.

The local church sponsors these classes or groups and supports them financially. The group is accountable to the pastor and local church board. Church board committees have the responsibility of developing programs. These groups may or may not become fully organized churches. However, they may come into membership of the sponsoring organized local church.

A. Multiworship Service

More than one worship service is held in the same facility. The difference in the services may be cultural but is usually language-based.

1. *Characteristics*
    a. The neighborhood consisted of four distinct racial, cultural, and/or language groups.
    b. The mother church wished to reach the neighborhood and its complex needs through the present structure and facilities.
    c. The building owned was adequate to have services

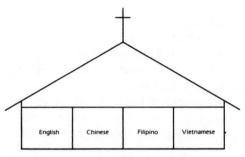

meet in several areas at the same time.

    d. Most of the young people and children spoke English.

    e. Immigration continued to feed the neighborhood with new people from the four main groups.

2. *Positive Ideas from the Model*

    a. Each congregation had its own pastor. The pastors were staff members of the whole church.

    b. Combined services were held as often as possible to promote unity.

    c. Financial responsibilities were established among the ethnic congregations. Payments were made not as rent but to help with the church budget.

    d. Representatives from each ethnic congregation served on the local church board of the governing body.

    e. All the congregations' Sunday Schools met at the same time. Youth and children of all the congregations met together when possible. Adults had elective classes including Bible study in their own language and English as a second language. In the ESL class, the Bible was used as a text, and studying English was combined with Bible truth.

    f. Each language group had classes during the week to train their laymen.

    g. Literature advertising the church was distributed in all four languages, thereby displaying to the community a spirit of unity in the church.

B. Multilanguage Classes

Many new immigrants are moving in who need to learn in their own language. Bible studies are offered to help meet their need.

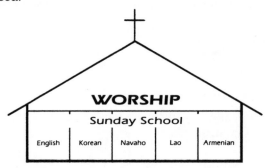

1. *Characteristics*
   a. Ten different language groups of immigrants and refugees had moved into this neighborhood.
   b. No other evangelical group was working with these groups.
   c. All groups seemed to coexist in the neighborhood with little friction.
   d. There was a strong desire among refugee and immigrant groups to make money in America. Most realized they must first learn English to get a good job.
   e. The sponsoring church had adequate space to have several classes meeting simultaneously.
2. *Positive Ideas for the Model*
   a. English as a second language classes were set up. U.S. Government literature on ethnics was used to understand the various cultures and language characteristics.
   b. The church was alerted to new immigrant arrivals by the local ethnic groups. Social services were set up to help with clothing, food, housing, and adjustment to a new country for these newcomers.

c. People graciously used their gifts to teach even when they had little training. This was especially true among senior citizens.

d. A missionary who had had many successful years overseas was recruited to supervise the program. His support came from churches in the area.

e. This model is now ready to start worship services in a few of the language groups that have been receptive to the gospel.

C. Multicultural

A multicultural church designs its services for a variety of cultural groups.

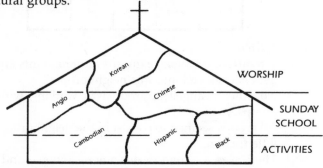

1. *Characteristics*

a. All cultures spoke a common language. This was not always their mother tongue.

b. Most of these cultural groups were moving upward socioeconomically and wished their children to learn and socialize in the language of the church. In this model that language was English.

c. The services tended to be less formal than average. Musical instruments, both stringed and brass, were often used.

d. Each cultural group was encouraged to promote social events and to keep an awareness of their heritage.

2. *Positive Ideas from the Model*
   a. The pastor stayed current on world news that involved the homelands of his new parishioners and used this material for his sermons.
   b. Classes were taught to help children born in America learn their own native language.
   c. Public worship services were carefully sprinkled with prayers and songs from the languages represented.
   d. The governing board was selected to include as many cultural groups as possible. This was done through careful nomination and not by designation of each group on the ballot. The result was representation without loss of a feeling of unity.
   e. Various cultural holidays and religious observations were recognized and celebrated when appropriate. Dressing in national costumes gave excitement to these special Sundays. Evangelism was encouraged by bringing family and friends to church dinners with emphasis on one particular ethnic food.

These models stand as examples of churches that were willing to build bridges and reach cross-culturally to others with the gospel. This is a golden opportunity era for the church in America. We must have an increasing number of churches who will develop their own guidelines and regulations in order to meet the challenges in their own neighborhoods.

7

Ethnic Church-planting Methods

There are some denominations, districts, and local churches that have creatively developed other methods for reaching cross-culturally to ethnic America. Most of these have resulted in new ethnic churches, although some were not originally designed for that purpose. The following are some ways that have been used successfully.

I. MISSION TEAMS

A. College Summer Ministry Teams

The district or local church recruits a group of college students who will volunteer their summer vacations for cross-cultural work. This work is designed by the sponsoring district or local church.

Several guidelines should be observed:

1. Good reading material is essential for the volunteers. These books should acquaint them with cross-cultural communication and the particular culture to be encountered.

2. Two five-day orientations are necessary. Subjects covered should include barriers to cross-cultural communication, culture shock, essential communications in the language

to be used, cultural values to be respected, and historical understanding of the area to be worked.

3. Selection of individuals should reflect the guidelines given in chapter 5 under "Special instructions prior to step 4." People are products of where they have been and what they have experienced. Everyone is influenced in some way by his background. Even a Christian can retain some feeling of racial prejudice.

Problems do arise in an encounter between people from different backgrounds. Mostly these problems are caused by preconceptions and prejudices on both sides. In cross-cultural evangelism it is necessary to use good judgment in team selection.

4. The teams should be closely supervised. They need listening ears and encouraging voices.

5. The sponsoring district or church should have a specific plan before the summer begins. Team members will work hard toward a goal that is clearly stated. They should have some free time also.

B. Construction Teams

For some time many churches have been sending building and improvement teams overseas. A growing number of churches, however, are beginning to help ethnic churches in the United States. It might be a small Mexican church on the Rio Grande, a Navajo church in Arizona, a Cambodian congregation in Minnesota, a Puerto Rican church in New York, or any one of many thousands across this nation.

People with construction skills are willing to pay their own way to the location. They also bring money and/or materials to pay for the project.

It is exciting that a smaller church can be involved. Overseas trips and the construction of a new church may have been beyond their ability. A nearby ethnic church, however, may require a short trip and only repair items to be purchased. When individuals in a local church get involved in helping others, it brings a new understanding and growth to all involved.

C. Youth Teams

The influx of immigrants and refugees has given countless opportunities for youth cultural exchange. Young people quickly pick up adult prejudices toward other cultures. By creating cross-cultural activities, most of these barriers will evaporate. These activities can range from sports events with an ethnic church across town to a bus ride to an Oklahoma Indian reservation. In all cases good planning is essential to assure the correct results.

II. SOCIAL SERVICES

In the fall of 1982 the Church of the Nazarene surveyed all of its 2,034 congregations in urbanized areas of the United States and Canada. Responses by mail and telephone were received from all pastors.

Pastors were asked to rate the extent of involvement by their congregation in each of 10 types of social work. Response ranged from 0 (not at all) to 10 (very much). The types of ministries and the number of congregations that ranked their involvement at a level of 6 or above are shown below:

Job Placement	81
Housing Placement	67
Medical Services	45
Day-care or Child Education	295
Adult Education	108
Clothing and Food Distribution	261
Immigrant Counseling	44
Alcohol/Drug Rehabilitation	79
Legal Counsel	53

A total of 621 or 31.1 percent of the churches indicated they were significantly involved in at least 1 of these 10 compassionate ministries. This is a number that was far above the expectation of the denominational leaders.

Social services ministries are being conducted as cross-cultural tools in most every area of need. But before beginning, one should know certain points:

1. Social services are expensive, and very little financial return will be received from those to whom one is ministering. It is difficult to raise funds among affluent Americans. Even those who are now successfully established in social work can tell of times when there was no money and very little moral support.

2. All of this does not change the fact that the church today must minister to the social and financial needs of America. It is not the government's place to provide these services. The Bible clearly places this responsibility on the church.

3. Most successful cross-cultural ministries that involve social services have been started and carried out by the leadership of one individual. It has been the sweat and tears of one man or woman who dedicated his or her life to see the work succeed. Without that person, the work would have died.

4. This is long-range work. Very few results are seen quickly.

5. Normal denominational statistics are not proper gauges by which to measure social services ministries.

There has been some debate in evangelical circles about evangelism and social services (see, in chapter 4, "Social Concern and Liberalism" section). This debate has had a tendency to alienate social workers from the mainstream of many denominations. They are, however, the best-qualified people to carry out a denominational movement back to the cross-cultural social needs of America. Their leadership and wisdom must not be overlooked.

When a social service ministry is conducting family

health care, housing placement, counseling, legal assistance, youth development, immigrant aid and training, or helping with any other need, the participants must be careful to include the following in their purpose:

1. To share the gospel in such a way that it meets the needs of the whole person.
2. To give encouragement to those who seek a closer and more personal relationship with God.
3. To be a resource and outreach for local churches in the area.
4. To participate in the development of indigenous Christian leadership.
5. To demonstrate and promote lasting racial and cultural reconciliation.
6. To promote the growth of strong and healthy Christian families.
7. To cooperate in the development of the local community economically, socially, and educationally.

III. ETHNIC RELIGIOUS TRAINING CENTERS

If the ethnic population of America is to be won to Christ, indigenous leadership must be developed. In attempting to accomplish this, several obstacles exist:

1. Many ethnics, because of job discrimination and language, are on a lower socioeconomic level than the average American. It is therefore difficult for them to afford today's cost of education.

2. Most of the religious education institutions of America are geared to the middle class. Lower-class individuals are ofttimes alienated and uncomfortable in this setting.

3. The level of English required in a college is usually beyond the ability of recent immigrants. The religious vocabulary, not learned on the street or out of an English textbook, is assumed in a first-year religion class.

4. Uprooting families for education is often impractical because of jobs, size of family, and lack of funds for moving.

5. Certain cultural distinctives and needs are not covered in a college program geared for the average American.

The answer to these problems does not lie in changing our campus classes to accommodate the diverse ethnic community. It does, however, call for branch education in the form used on mission fields—theological education by extension. This should be regulated, governed, and accredited by existing institutions. It would be helpful if education is largely in the language of the culture, if teachers are available. The teaching otherwise should take on a style that is basic in its English without lowering the content level. The ideal is a combination of basic English and the native language, with heavy instruction on learning English as a second language.

This approach has several advantages:

1. Each community where an ethnic population exists can have limited training.

2. Local churches can house these centers, saving building cost and maintenance.

3. Local pastors with proper education could be used as teachers and administrators. Salaries would be minimal since their housing and expenses would already be covered by their local church. Care should be exercised in the selection of these individuals.

4. Ethnic individuals called to preach would not have to uproot their families.

5. Special courses in the ethnic language needed (or cultural distinctives) could be taught by area personnel or video presentation.

The training centers, like their mother institutions, would strive to equip their students for the exercise of the Christian ministry, providing an integral education in accordance with biblical principles. This education should include spiritual, intellectual, and practical preparation designed to enable the student to serve the Lord with effective excellence.

IV. ENGLISH AS A SECOND LANGUAGE (ESL)

Missionaries overseas have long seen the value of teaching English as a second (or foreign) language. ESL has been used as a tool to attract non-Christian people into a Christian setting. Since the Bible is written in good English and is available in various levels of vocabulary, it has been an excellent book to teach to these classes.

With the influx of ethnics to America (described in chapter 2), churches and denominations are beginning to see the benefit of this tool "at home."

English is an important element to one's successful adjustment to America. The church has a responsibility to aid in this adjustment period. By setting up classes in English, the church helps immigrants and refugees and provides an excellent evangelistic tool.

The following resources should be investigated:

1. *A Dictionary of the Bible and Christian Doctrine in Everyday English*

Using a 2,500-word vocabulary, a group of biblical and theological scholars have teamed with ESL experts to produce a basic English dictionary of biblical and theological terminology. The volume contains simple definitions of key terms and is available from Nazarene Publishing House, P.O. Box 527, Kansas City, MO 64141.

2. *Sunday School Literature*

Some denominations are presently producing adult Sunday School literature in English with a limited vocabulary. Write to the publishing house of your denomination or the supplier of your Sunday School literature and inquire.

3. *Ministerial and Lay Training*

Often refugees are fleeing countries where governments have not permitted Christian literature to be written or published. Since there is no material in their language available to train them, simple English must be used. Once again check with your publishing house to see what is available. (Nazarene Publishing House does have some texts available.)

V. SPONSORING REFUGEES

An astounding number of people are still in refugee camps around the world. Each year thousands of families are sponsored by individuals in America. One of the placement agencies is World Relief, an arm of the National Association of Evangelicals (NAE). Families placed in Christian homes have many times found Christ and become the nucleus for an evangelical work among that group.

Conclusion

Thinking Globally While Acting Locally

Ray Bakke's question is repeated here: "Why is God internationalizing the cities of the United States?" Although this query provides religious philosophers with material for a timeless debate, the following reasons will offer a clue:

1. *To Close the Back Door of Missions*

Global movement is part of the reality of the 1980s. War, revolution, economic reversals, famine, and curiosity have combined with the convenience of fast transportation to create a mobile world. What overseas missions have accomplished in the last few decades must not be lost in the migration of these Christians. The United States, with church buildings and adequate resources in almost every county and city, is better equipped to house and nurture these mission products than any other nation of the world.

2. *To Bring a New Awareness of Real Mission Work to the United States*

The Great Commission starts with Jerusalem (our own neighborhood) and spreads to Samaria (our local cross-cultural challenge) and then to the world. Many of us find very little distinction today between our "Jerusalem" and our "Samaria." There is a new challenge for "missions at home" settling over the church of America. We can no longer feel fulfilled in paying for mission work to be done by others. Our mission field (even to other cultures and languages) is right next door.

3. *To Create Beautiful Examples of Church Unity*

With the Trinity as our example, we are seeing a growing number of churches allowing their buildings to be used by more than one language group. Yet each congregation functions within its own culture and for its own purpose. The unity admonished by Paul in Romans 12; 14; 15; 1 Corinthians 1; Philippians 1; 2; and 3 is obviously displayed.

4. *To Evangelize People Who Cannot Be Reached in Their Native Culture*

There are not enough missionaries presently commissioned to reach all remote areas of the world. But even if there were personnel ready to serve in every country, many nations are still unavailable because of political restrictions. So it is no wonder that God is bringing these people to us! Often when they reach the United States they are concentrated in one area, thus enhancing the effectiveness of an evangelistic effort. The religious culture of Americans, combined with the social, emotional, and economic needs of the immigrants, increases their receptivity to Christianity.

5. *To Establish an Ethnic Pool of Potential Missionaries*

With prayer and proper instruction, an indigenous work force is available for virtually every country of the world. It is their country, their language, and their culture. Who is better qualified to win their own people? The potential is limitless.

GOD is internationalizing the United States! But what will be our response? By conserving immigrating Christians, evangelizing and training ethnic America, a launching pad can be established whereby the entire WORLD can be reached with the gospel of Jesus Christ. We must think globally while we act locally.

Appendix

Ethnic Population Clusters

American Indian

Population	Metropolitan Statistical Area
94,706	Los Angeles-Anaheim-Riverside, Calif.
38,282	San Francisco-Oakland-San Jose, Calif.
34,158	Tulsa, Okla.
26,339	New York-Northern New Jersey-Long Island, N.Y.-N.J.-Conn.
26,294	Oklahoma City, Okla.
23,635	Phoenix, Ariz.
22,355	Seattle-Tacoma, Wash.
17,126	Minneapolis-St. Paul, Minn.-Wis.
16,187	San Diego, Calif.
15,445	Detroit-Ann Arbor, Mich.
15,230	Tucson, Ariz.
13,600	Sacramento, Calif.
13,471	Dallas-Fort Worth, Tex.
13,432	Chicago-Gary-Lake County, Ill.-Ind.-Wis.
10,946	Albuquerque, N.Mex.
10,595	Denver-Boulder, Colo.
9,650	Portland-Vancouver, Oreg.-Wash.
8,907	Houston-Galveston-Brazoria, Tex.
8,120	Philadelphia-Trenton-Wilmington, Pa.-N.J.-Del.-Md.
7,768	Washington, D.C.-Md.-Va.
7,253	Milwaukee-Racine, Wis.
7,162	Buffalo-Niagara Falls, N.Y.
6,828	Fort Smith, Ark.-Okla.
6,669	Yakima, Wash.
6,628	Kansas City, Mo.-Kans.

Asian Indian

Population	Metropolitan Statistical Area
85,808	New York-Northern New Jersey-Long Island, N.Y.-N.J.-Conn.
34,080	Chicago-Gary-Lake County, Ill.-Ind.-Wis.
26,535	Los Angeles-Anaheim-Riverside, Calif.
19,259	San Francisco-Oakland-San Jose, Calif.
15,814	Washington, D.C.-Md.-Va.
13,426	Philadelphia-Trenton-Wilmington, Pa.-N.J.-Del.-Md.
12,257	Houston-Galveston-Brazoria, Tex.
11,757	Detroit-Ann Arbor, Mich.
6,875	Boston-Lawrence-Salem-Lowell-Brockton, Mass.
5,512	Cleveland-Akron-Lorain, Ohio
5,089	Dallas-Fort Worth, Tex.
4,891	Miami-Fort Lauderdale, Fla.
4,152	Baltimore, Md.
3,466	Pittsburgh-Beaver Valley, Pa.
2,928	Minneapolis-St. Paul, Minn.-Wis.
2,786	Yuba City, Calif.
2,757	Seattle-Tacoma, Wash.
2,734	St. Louis-East St. Louis-Alton, Mo.-Ill.
2,638	Atlanta, Ga.
2,323	Sacramento, Calif.
2,097	San Diego, Calif.
2,068	Buffalo-Niagara Falls, N.Y.
2,034	Hartford-New Britain-Middletown-Bristol, Conn.
1,946	Denver-Boulder, Colo.
1,935	Cincinnati-Hamilton, Ohio-Ky.-Ind.

Black

Population	Metropolitan Statistical Area
2,825,444	New York-Northern New Jersey-Long Island, N.Y.-N.J.-Conn.
1,557,021	Chicago-Gary-Lake County, Ill.-Ind.-Wis.
1,057,876	Los Angeles-Anaheim-Riverside, Calif.
1,031,824	Philadelphia-Trenton-Wilmington, Pa.-N.J.-Del.-Md.
919,683	Detroit-Ann Arbor, Mich.
870,428	Washington, D.C.-Md.-Va.
563,365	Houston-Galveston-Brazoria, Tex.
559,596	Baltimore, Md.
525,507	Atlanta, Ga.
467,823	San Francisco-Oakland-San Jose, Calif.
425,538	Cleveland-Akron-Lorain, Ohio
416,608	Dallas-Fort Worth, Tex.
409,078	New Orleans, La.
407,213	St. Louis-East St. Louis-Alton, Mo.-Ill.
394,704	Miami-Fort Lauderdale, Fla.
363,943	Memphis, Tenn.-Ark.-Miss.
326,115	Norfolk-Virginia Beach-Newport News, Va.
240,204	Birmingham, Ala.
221,474	Richmond-Petersburg, Va.
194,296	Charlotte-Gastonia-Rock Hill, N.C.-S.C.
185,651	Cincinnati-Hamilton, Ohio-Ky.-Ind.
181,416	Pittsburgh-Beaver Valley, Pa.
179,477	Kansas City, Mo.-Kans.
173,269	Boston-Lawrence-Salem-Lowell-Brockton, Mass.
164,662	Milwaukee-Racine, Wis.

Chinese

Population	Metropolitan Statistical Area
169,691	San Francisco-Oakland-San Jose, Calif.
159,073	New York-Northern New Jersey-Long Island, N.Y.-N.J.-Conn.
115,247	Los Angeles-Anaheim-Riverside, Calif.
52,301	Honolulu, Hawaii
25,545	Chicago-Gary-Lake County, Ill.-Ind.-Wis.
22,600	Boston-Lawrence-Salem-Lowell-Brockton, Mass.
18,402	Washington, D.C.-Md.-Va.
15,598	Sacramento, Calif.
15,270	Seattle-Tacoma, Wash.
14,235	Houston-Galveston-Brazoria, Tex.
12,263	Philadelphia-Trenton-Wilmington, Pa.-N.J.-Del.-Md.
8,618	San Diego, Calif.
8,203	Detroit-Ann Arbor, Mich.
6,826	Miami-Fort Lauderdale, Fla.
5,642	Dallas-Fort Worth, Tex.
5,342	Portland-Vancouver, Oreg.-Wash.
4,392	Stockton, Calif.
4,237	Baltimore, Md.
4,185	Phoenix, Ariz.
4,034	Cleveland-Akron-Lorain, Ohio
3,516	Fresno, Calif.
3,311	Denver-Boulder, Colo.
3,218	Minneapolis-St. Paul, Minn.-Wis.
3,132	St. Louis-East St. Louis-Alton, Mo.-Ill.
2,544	Pittsburgh-Beaver Valley, Pa.

Cuban

Filipino

Population	Metropolitan Statistical Area
139,676	San Francisco-Oakland-San Jose, Calif.
125,565	Los Angeles-Anaheim-Riverside, Calif.
96,421	Honolulu, Hawaii
54,690	New York-Northern New Jersey-Long Island, N.Y.-N.J.-Conn.
47,106	San Diego, Calif.
42,548	Chicago-Gary-Lake County, Ill.-Ind.-Wis.
18,945	Seattle-Tacoma, Wash.
13,091	Washington, D.C.-Md.-Va.
12,297	Norfolk-Virginia Beach-Newport News, Va.
8,735	Stockton, Calif.
8,719	Philadelphia-Trenton-Wilmington, Pa.-N.J.-Del.-Md.
8,595	Detroit-Ann Arbor, Mich.
8,269	Salinas-Seaside-Monterey, Calif.
8,079	Sacramento, Calif.
6,079	Houston-Galveston-Brazoria, Tex.
4,703	Jacksonville, Fla.
4,070	Baltimore, Md.
3,483	Portland-Vancouver, Oreg.-Wash.
3,476	Cleveland-Akron-Lorain, Ohio
3,305	Santa Barbara-Santa Maria-Lompoc, Calif.
3,091	Visalia-Tulare-Porterville, Calif.
2,876	Dallas-Fort Worth, Tex.
2,773	St. Louis-East St. Louis-Alton, Mo.-Ill.
2,641	Miami-Fort Lauderdale, Fla.
2,569	Charleston, S.C.

Japanese

Population	Metropolitan Statistical Area
190,218	Honolulu, Hawaii
147,623	Los Angeles-Anaheim-Riverside, Calif.
68,585	San Francisco-Oakland-San Jose, Calif.
29,934	New York-Northern New Jersey-Long Island, N.Y.-N.J.-Conn.
21,764	Seattle-Tacoma, Wash.
16,301	Chicago-Gary-Lake County, Ill.-Ind.-Wis.
14,955	Sacramento, Calif.
13,110	San Diego, Calif.
7,778	Denver-Boulder, Colo.
6,487	Washington, D.C.-Md.-Va.
6,360	Fresno, Calif.
5,005	Portland-Vancouver, Oreg.-Wash.
4,552	Philadelphia-Trenton-Wilmington, Pa.-N.J.-Del.-Md.
4,370	Salt Lake City-Ogden, Utah
4,323	Stockton, Calif.
4,185	Salinas-Seaside-Monterey, Calif.
3,923	Detroit-Ann Arbor, Mich.
3,424	Boston-Lawrence-Salem-Lowell-Brockton, Mass.
3,352	Houston-Galveston-Brazoria, Tex.
2,817	Dallas-Fort Worth, Tex.
2,610	Phoeniz, Ariz.
2,507	Santa Barbara-Santa Maria-Lompoc, Calif.
2,413	Minneapolis-St. Paul, Minn.-Wis.
2,231	Cleveland-Akron-Lorain, Ohio
1,704	Las Vegas, Nev.

Korean

Population	Metropolitan Statistical Area
74,142	Los Angeles-Anaheim-Riverside, Calif.
38,297	New York-Northern New Jersey-Long Island, N.Y.-N.J.-Conn.
21,973	Chicago-Gary-Lake County, Ill.-Ind.-Wis.
18,870	San Francisco-Oakland-San Jose, Calif.
17,913	Washington, D.C.-Md.-Va.
16,566	Honolulu, Hawaii
10,930	Philadelphia-Trenton-Wilmington, Pa.-N.J.-Del.-Md.
10,438	Seattle-Tacoma, Wash.
6,400	Baltimore, Md.
5,004	Detroit-Ann Arbor, Mich.
4,989	Minneapolis-St. Paul, Minn.-Wis.
3,782	Portland-Vancouver, Oreg.-Wash.
3,684	Boston-Lawrence-Salem-Lowell-Brockton, Mass.
3,553	Houston-Galveston-Brazoria, Tex.
3,131	Dallas-Fort Worth, Tex.
3,088	Denver-Boulder, Colo.
2,810	San Diego, Calif.
2,654	Atlanta, Ga.
2,613	Salinas-Seaside-Monterey, Calif.
2,115	Cleveland-Akron-Lorain, Ohio
2,107	Killeen-Temple, Tex.
1,911	St. Louis-East St. Louis-Alton, Mo.-Ill.
1,762	Las Vegas, Nev.
1,742	Sacramento, Calif.
1,698	Colorado Springs, Colo.

Mexican

Puerto Rican

Population	Metropolitan Statistical Area
1,158,112	New York-Northern New Jersey-Long Island, N.Y.-N.J-Conn.
139,924	Chicago-Gary-Lake County, Ill.-Ind.-Wis.
102,197	Philadelphia-Trenton-Wilmington, Pa.-N.J.-Del.-Md.
55,477	Miami-Fort Lauderdale, Fla.
48,614	Los Angeles-Anaheim-Riverside, Calif.
41,377	Boston-Lawrence-Salem-Lowell-Brockton, Mass.
34,381	Hartford-New Britain-Middletown-Bristol, Conn.
28,003	San Francisco-Oakland-San Jose, Calif.
23,429	Cleveland-Akron-Lorain, Ohio
20,418	New Haven-Waterbury-Meriden, Conn.
20,236	Springfield, Mass.
13,817	Honolulu, Hawaii
13,180	Rochester, N.Y.
10,847	Tampa-St. Petersburg-Clearwater, Fla.
10,317	Allentown-Bethlehem, Pa.-N.J.
9,967	Washington, D.C.-Md.-Va.
9,401	Worcester-Fitchburg-Leominster, Mass.
9,325	Milwaukee-Racine, Wis.
9,285	Orlando, Fla.
8,729	Buffalo-Niagara Falls, N.Y.
7,764	Detroit-Ann Arbor, Mich.
7,423	Reading, Pa.
6,731	Lancaster, Pa.
6,643	Atlantic City, N.J.
5,484	San Diego, Calif.

Vietnamese

Population	Metropolitan Statistical Area
47,993	Los Angeles-Anaheim-Riverside, Calif.
22,172	San Francisco-Oakland-San Jose, Calif.
9,967	Washington, D.C.-Md.-Va.
8,084	New Orleans, La.
7,564	San Diego, Calif.
6,358	New York-Northern New Jersey-Long Island, N.Y.-N.J.-Conn.
5,859	Seattle-Tacoma, Wash.
5,348	Dallas-Fort Worth, Tex.
4,878	Portland-Vancouver, Oreg.-Wash.
4,706	Chicago-Gary-Lake County, Ill.-Ind.-Wis.
4,023	Philadelphia-Trenton-Wilmington, Pa.-N.J.-Del.-Md.
3,685	Houston-Galveston-Brazoria, Tex.
3,613	Minneapolis-St. Paul, Minn.-Wis.
3,251	Honolulu, Hawaii
2,810	Sacramento, Calif.
2,502	Denver-Boulder, Colo.
2,227	Oklahoma City, Okla.
2,199	Boston-Lawrence-Salem-Lowell-Brockton, Mass.
2,032	Beaumont-Port Arthur, Tex.
1,940	Wichita, Kans.
1,676	Grand Rapids, Mich.
1,639	Kansas City, Mo.-Kans.
1,602	Salt Lake City-Ogden, Utah
1,297	San Antonio, Tex.
1,285	Tampa-St. Petersburg-Clearwater, Fla.

Western

Population   *Metropolitan Statistical Area*

Aleut

1,539	Anchorage, Alaska
1,128	Los Angeles-Anaheim-Riverside, Calif.

Eskimo

3,297	Anchorage, Alaska
1,077	Los Angeles-Anaheim-Riverside, Calif.

Guamanian

6,154	San Francisco-Oakland-San Jose, Calif.
5,400	Los Angeles-Anaheim-Riverside, Calif.
3,650	San Diego, Calif.
1,470	Honolulu, Hawaii
1,027	New York-Northern New Jersey-Long Island, N.Y.-N.J.-Conn.

Hawaiian

81,868	Honolulu, Hawaii
10,335	Los Angeles-Anaheim-Riverside, Calif.
7,744	San Francisco-Oakland-San Jose, Calif.
2,704	San Diego, Calif.
1,957	Seattle-Tacoma, Wash.
1,947	New York-Northern New Jersey-Long Island, N.Y.-N.J.-Conn.
1,020	Sacramento, Calif.

Samoan

13,975	Honolulu, Hawaii
9,866	Los Angeles-Anaheim-Riverside, Calif.
4,584	San Francisco-Oakland-San Jose, Calif.
2,699	San Diego, Calif.
1,565	Seattle-Tacoma, Wash.